DK EYEWITNESS TRAVEL

TOP
ISRAEL
& PETRA

VANESSA BETTS

526 631 46 8

Penguin Random House

Top 10 Israel and Petra Highlights

The Top 10 of Everything

CONTENTS

Israel and Petra Area by Area

Streetsmart

Within each Top 10 list in this book, no hierarchy of quality or popularity is implied. All 10 are, in the editor's opinion, of roughly equal merit.

Throughout this book, floors are referred to in accordance with American usage; i.e., the "first floor" is at ground level.

Front cover and spine *Jerusalem, Yerushalayim, Dome of the Rock, The Temple Mount*
Back cover *A beautiful day at the Monastery (Ad-Deir), Petra*
Title page *The Church of the Holy Sepulchre, one of Jerusalem's holiest sites*

Welcome to
Israel and Petra

Holy sites and beachside hedonism, ancient ruins and Bauhaus buildings, desert oases and Galilean springs – Israel and Petra combine the age-old and the high-tech, the earthy and the spiritual. Add excellent cuisine and wines and you have a feast for the senses, mind, and spirit. With Eyewitness Top 10 Israel & Petra, it is yours to explore.

In Jerusalem, the three great Abrahamic faiths connect with their ancient sources. Jews the world over pray toward Jerusalem, and when here flock to the **Western Wall**, a remnant of the Holy Temple that once stood on the **Temple Mount**. For many Christians, no site is more sacred than the **Church of the Holy Sepulchre**, where it is believed that Jesus was crucified, buried, and resurrected. In nearby **Bethlehem**, the Church of the Nativity marks what many believe is Jesus' birthplace. Muslims venerate Al-Aqsa Mosque and the Dome of the Rock, both on Jerusalem's **Temple Mount** (Al-Haram ash-Sharif). The city's **Israel Museum** displays artifacts that bring ancient times to life.

Dynamic **Tel Aviv-Jaffa**, an economic powerhouse, has fine-sand Mediterranean beaches, as well as excellent museums, shopping, and nightlife. Up the coast in **Haifa**, a model of Jewish-Arab coexistence, the incredible **Baha'i Gardens** adorn the slopes of Mount Carmel.

Whether you're coming for a weekend or a week, our Top 10 guide brings together the best of everything that Israel and Petra have to offer, from the mineral-rich waters of the **Dead Sea** and the ancient synagogues of the **Sea of Galilee** to the incredible ruined Nabataean city of **Petra**. The guide has useful tips throughout, from seeking out what's free to avoiding the crowds, plus eight easy-to-follow itineraries, designed to tie together a clutch of sights in a short space of time. Add inspiring photography and detailed maps, and you've got the essential pocket-sized travel companion. **Enjoy the book, and enjoy Israel and Petra**.

Clockwise from top: Dome of the Rock, Design Museum Holon, Jaffa Port, the Monastery at Petra, ancient church mosaic in Petra, shops at Jerusalem's Cardo Maximus, Yad Vashem

Exploring Israel and Petra

Whether you're interested in biblical archeology, hiking through awe-inspiring landscapes, or relaxing on the beach, you can easily spend months exploring all that Israel and Petra – despite their small size – have to offer. But you can also pack a great deal into a week-long trip, starting with two days in the holy city of Jerusalem.

Two Days in Jerusalem

Day ❶

MORNING

Start at the Citadel *(see p67)* at Jaffa Gate, then head to the incense-filled **Church of the Holy Sepulchre** *(see pp12–13)* in the Old City's Christian Quarter. Walk through the Muslim Quarter's souk (market) and the Jewish Quarter to the **Western Wall** *(see pp16–17)*. Enter the **Temple Mount** *(see pp14–15)* via the Moors' Gate. Non-Muslims can only admire the elaborately tiled, gold-domed **Dome of the Rock** and **Al-Aqsa Mosque** from the outside.

AFTERNOON

Visit the excavations at the **City of David** *(see p70)*, where you can splash through **Hezekiah's Tunnel** *(see p48)*. Then cross Kidron Valley to the **Mount of Olives** *(see p68)*, with its landmark churches and stunning views.

The Treasury, Petra

Day ❷

MORNING

At the **Israel Museum** *(see pp18–21)*, walk through the Archeology Wing, with its treasures from ancient Israel and neighboring civilizations, then see the Dead Sea Scrolls. Stroll through the Billy Rose Art Garden on your way to see paintings by Rembrandt and Monet.

Key

━━ Two-day itinerary
━━ Seven-day itinerary

AFTERNOON

Absorb the testimonies and artifacts at the museum at **Yad Vashem** *(see p40)*. A Children's Memorial recalls the 1.5 million Jewish children who died during the Holocaust; a crypt near the Hall of Remembrance holds the ashes of death-camp victims.

Seven Days in Israel and Petra

Days **1** and **2**

Follow the two-day itinerary for Jerusalem.

Day **3**

Now head to Manger Square in **Bethlehem** (*see pp26–7*); bow through the impossibly low front door to enter the **Church of the Nativity**. Visit the adjacent **St Catherine's Church** and the **Milk Grotto** before checking out the **Old Market**, which sells fruit, vegetables, and snacks. Then head to Beit Sahour, site of the **Shepherd's Fields** and two churches.

Day **4**

By car or on a tour, head to the **Dead Sea** (*see pp96–101*). Visit **Qumran National Park** (*see p98*), where the Dead Sea Scrolls were found, and **Ein Gedi Nature Reserve** (*see p97*) for a hike in a lush desert oasis. Visit the Masada Museum before climbing or taking the cable car to the top of **Masada** (*see pp30–31*). Stop at **Ein Bokek** (*see p46*) for a dip in the sea.

Day **5**

Enter Jordan at the Yitzhak Rabin/ Wadi Araba border crossing. From Wadi Musa, walk or ride through **the Siq** (*see pp34–5*) until the ancient city of **Petra** (*see pp102–5*) is spectacularly revealed. Admire the Treasury and other grand Nabataean edifices. Head back to Israel and drive part of the way to **Tel Aviv-Jaffa** (*see pp80–87*).

The holy Dome of the Rock shrine in Jerusalem is open only to Muslims.

Day **6**

From the ancient city of **Jaffa** (*see p82*), with its many art galleries, stroll north along the **Tel Aviv-Jaffa Beachfront** (*see pp28–9*), pausing for a drink at a beach café. Have lunch at **Tel Aviv Port** (*see p81*). Then cross the Yarkon River to visit the **Eretz Israel Museum** (*see p40*) and **Beit HaTfutsot (Museum of the Jewish People)** (*see p41*) on the campus of Tel Aviv university. Don't forget to check out the Bauhaus architecture (*see p84*) before enjoying a gourmet dinner in central Tel Aviv.

Day **7**

Head to **Tiberias** (*see p92*) and drive north along the shore of the **Sea of Galilee** (*see pp32–3*) to **Magdala** (*see p33*), hometown of Mary Magdalene, and then admire a wooden fishing boat from the time of Jesus at Kibbutz Ginosar (*see p32*). Continue around the shoreline, stopping at the **Mount of Beatitudes** and **Tabgha** (*see p32*), and the synagogues of **Capernaum** and **Korazim** (*see p33*). End the day at **Kursi** (*see p33*).

Jaffa, on the shores of the Mediterranean, is one of the world's oldest ports.

Top 10 Israel and Petra Highlights

The golden Dome of the Rock shrine on Jerusalem's Temple Mount

TOP 10 Israel and Petra Highlights

This tiny strip of land, holy to the world's three great monotheistic religions, has a wealth of history, monuments, ruins, and places of worship to discover. The region also offers extraordinary natural beauty, from the forested slopes of the Galilee, to Mediterranean white-sand beaches, and the desert vistas of the Negev and Petra.

1 Church of the Holy Sepulchre

The holiest church for Catholics and Orthodox Christians is built on the site where, tradition says, Jesus was crucified, buried, and resurrected (see pp12–13).

2 Temple Mount

Site of Judaism's First and Second temples, Jerusalem's Temple Mount (Al-Haram ash-Sharif) has been topped by the spectacular Dome of the Rock since the 7th century (see pp14–15).

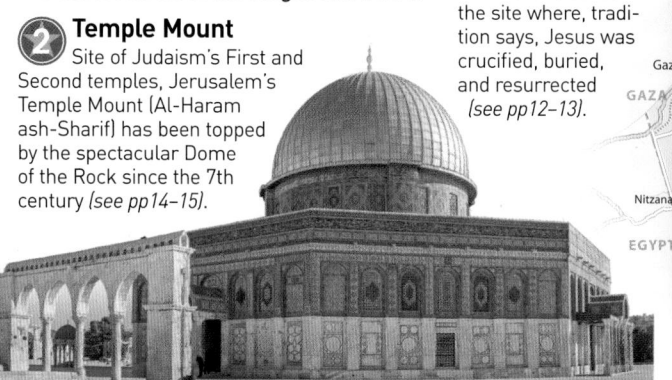

Gaz
GAZA
Nitzana
EGYPT

3 Western Wall

Judaism's holiest place of prayer, the Western Wall is part of the Temple Mount's retaining wall, built by Herod the Great in the 1st century BC (see pp16–17).

4 Israel Museum

The Israel Museum houses a vast collection of art, archeology, and Jewish artifacts, plus the iconic Shrine of the Book displaying the Dead Sea Scrolls (see pp18–21).

5 Haifa

A bastion of Jewish-Arab coexistence, this port city enjoys spectacular sea views from Mount Carmel, especially from the exquisite Baha'i Gardens (see pp24–5)

kilometers 50
miles 50

LEBANON

Banias
Nahariyya
Akko
Safed • Katzrin
Haifa **5** Tiberias **9** Sea of Galilee
Nazareth
Afula
Beit She'an
Caesarea
Khadera
Netanya
Nablus
WEST BANK

7 Tel Aviv-Jaffa Beachfront
Ramallah
Ashdod Jerusalem
see inset map
Ashkelon **6** Bethlehem
Hebron Dead Sea
Ein Gedi
Arad **8** Masada
Be'er Sheva Ein Bokek
Mamshit
ISRAEL
Sde Boker
Mitzpe Ramon
JORDAN
Be'er Menukha
10 The Siq, Petra
Yotvata
Eilat • Aqaba

Jerusalem Old City
SULTAN SULEIMAN
VIA DOLOROSA
OLD CITY
1 **2**
4 DAVID ST CHAIN ST **3**
2.5 miles (4 km)
HURVA SQUARE
0 meters 500
0 yards 500

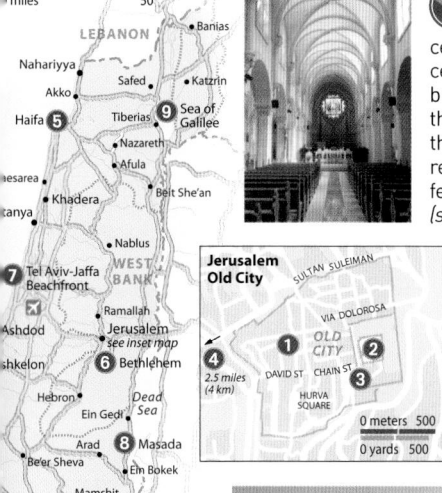

6 Bethlehem
A major pilgrimage center since the 4th century AD, Jesus' birthplace – centered on the imposing Church of the Nativity – even today retains the small-town feel of centuries past (see pp26–7).

7 Tel Aviv-Jaffa Beachfront
The dynamic city of Tel Aviv-Jaffa has miles of glorious seafront, where you can swim, dine, or visit Old Jaffa's galleries (see pp28–9).

Masada **8**
Perched atop a plateau, this fortress is where, in the 1st century AD, around 1,000 Jewish rebels chose suicide over surrender to Roman rule (see pp30–31).

9 Sea of Galilee
Jesus spent most of his ministry around the shores of Israel's largest freshwater lake, now peppered with ancient synagogues and Christian pilgrimage sites (see pp32–3).

The Siq, Petra **10**
Known as the Siq, the narrow gorge that leads visitors to Petra offers a spectacular and dramatic intro-duction to the "rose-red city half as old as time" (see pp34–5).

TOP 10 ⭐ Church of the Holy Sepulchre

Venerated as the site of the crucifixion and resurrection of Jesus, this is, for many, the holiest venue in Christendom. The first church was built here for Emperor Constantine in AD 326. Destroyed in AD 614 by the Persians and by the Fatimid Sultan Hakim in 1009, it was rebuilt by the Crusaders between 1114 and 1170. Having survived fire and earthquake, it is now administered by six Christian denominations.

1 Ethiopian Monastery

Cells on the roof of the Chapel of St. Helena have been occupied by the Ethiopians since the 17th century. A door leads down to the Ethiopian chapel, through a Coptic Chapel, and down to the Parvis.

NEED TO KNOW

MAP P4 ■ The Christian Quarter, Old City ■ (02) 626 7000 ■ Light Rail to City Hall, or Egged bus 60 to Jaffa Gate

Open summer: 5am–9pm (till 8pm in Oct); winter: 4am–7pm daily

■ There is only one entrance into the Church of the Holy Sepulchre, via the main courtyard. Wheelchair users will not be able to enter Christ's Tomb, Golgotha, or the side chapels, but can safely negotiate the main area of the church.

■ There are several restaurants and cafés at the Muristan (see p70), only a minute's walk from the main entrance.

2 Parvis

This courtyard is lined with tiny chapels belonging to various denominations **(above)**. The imposing façade of the church is Crusader, with marble pillars and fine stonework.

3 Chapel of Adam

The lower section of the Rock of Golgotha can be seen here. The fissure is believed to have been caused by an earthquake after the crucifixion.

4 Chapel of St. Helena

This Armenian chapel **(right)** dates back to Crusader times. The walls of the steps down are marked with crosses carved by early pilgrims.

7 Christ's Tomb

At the heart of the church, a marble shrine known as the Edicule encloses the place where Jesus' body is believed to have been laid after his crucifixion **(left)**. In 2016, a conservation team lifted the covering limestone slab for the first time in almost 500 years.

> **THE HOLY FIRE**
>
> At Easter, the Greek Orthodox celebrate Holy Saturday, when the Miracle of the Holy Fire symbolizes the resurrection of Christ. The Patriarch leads the ceremony, which sees an unlit candle burst into flames inside Christ's Tomb. This miraculous candle is then used to light the candles of worshippers. Holy Fire falls on April 7 in 2018 and April 27 in 2019.

9 Syrian Chapel

Accessed through the rear wall of the Rotunda, this dilapidated chapel contains Jewish rock-cut tombs dating from 100 BC–AD 100. The candlelit tombs give an impression of how Christ's burial place might have looked.

5 Golgotha

Well-worn steps lead to the Rock of Golgotha, which commemorates the site of the crucifixion with glorious altars and glinting mosaics. It is possible to touch the rock itself, situated beneath the Greek Orthodox altar **(above)**.

8 Catholikon Dome

Decorated with an image of Christ, the Catholikon Dome covers the central nave of the Crusader church. The omphalos (literally "navel"), a stone basin beneath the dome, reflects the medieval belief that this was the center of the world.

6 The Rotunda

The main dome, decorated with a 12-pointed star and pierced by an oculus, rises above the Rotunda. The colonnade was rebuilt after 1808, but two pillars still remain from the original basilica.

10 Stone of Unction

This stone marks the spot where Christ's body was anointed and wrapped before burial. The 12th-century stone was destroyed in the fire of 1808. A smooth limestone slab installed in 1810 marks its original location **(above)**.

📸10 ⭐ Temple Mount

The focal point of Jerusalem for over 3,000 years, the Temple Mount was the site of Solomon's First Temple and its replacement, the Second Temple. Rebuilt in the 1st century BC by Herod the Great, the complex (from where Jesus is said to have expelled the merchants and moneychangers) was destroyed by the Romans in AD 70. The Mount remained derelict until the arrival of Islam in the 7th century, when the golden Dome of the Rock was built and the Mount became known to Muslims as Al-Haram ash-Sharif (the Noble Sanctuary).

Temple Mount

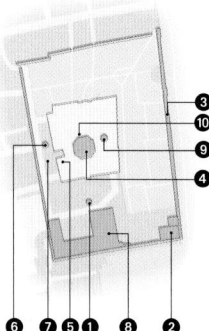

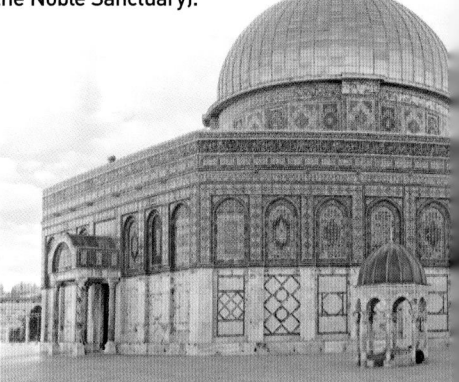

1 Al-Kas Fountain

The largest of the ablution fountains still operational on the Mount, the 14th-century Al-Kas is carved from a single block of stone.

2 Solomon's Stables

Part of the underground vaulting system **(above)** built by Herod to support the Second Temple, this structure became a mosque in 1996. It can hold 10,000 worshippers.

3 Golden Gate

Jewish tradition states that the Messiah will enter Jerusalem through this Herodian portal. Walled up in the 7th century, the gate has remained closed ever since.

NEED TO KNOW

MAP Q4 ■ Entrance via Moors' Gate, next to the Western Wall Plaza ■ (02) 622 6250 ■ Egged buses 1 and 3

Open summer: 7:30–11am & 1:30–2:30pm Sun–Thu; winter: 7:30–10am & 12:30–1.30pm Sun–Thu

■ Non-Muslims must enter through the Moors' Gate but they can exit via any open gate. Non-Muslims cannot enter the Dome of the Rock or Al-Aqsa Mosque.

■ Jewish religious law prohibits Jews from visiting, while Israeli secular law forbids Jews from praying here.

4 Dome of the Rock

Built in AD 688–91 by Caliph Abd al-Malik, this shrine **(below)** is one of the world's great architectural glories. A synthesis of Byzantine and Classical styles, the octagonal structure was built with mathematical precision to enshrine the Holy Rock within.

7 Ashrafiyya Madrasa

One of several Islamic colleges on the platform, the Ashrafiyya was built in 1482 by Qaitbey and is a masterpiece of Islamic design. The doorway incorporates bands of colored stone, stalactite carvings, and interlocking "joggled" stones.

INSIDE THE DOME OF THE ROCK

The interior of this shrine (closed to non-Muslims) is lavishly decorated with inscriptions and floral motifs. At the center of the octagon stands the Holy Rock, from where Mohammad is believed to have begun his Night Journey, leaving his footprint in the corner. For Jews, the Rock is associated both with Abraham's sacrifice of Isaac and as the site of the Holy of Holies.

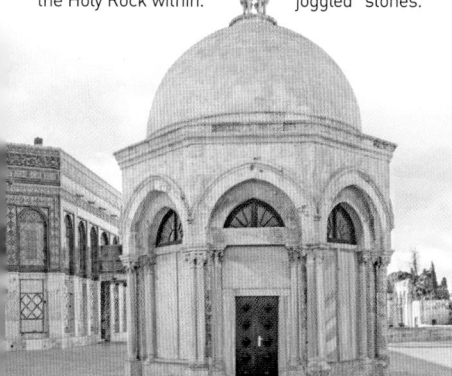

9 Dome of the Chain

Supported by 17 columns **(below)**, the structure's purpose, remains a mystery. The 13th-century tiling on the interior is as exquisite as that inside the Dome of the Rock.

5 Minbar of Burhan al-Din

This delicate *minbar* (pulpit) by the south *qanatir* is exquisitely carved, and includes some delicate Crusader sculpture. It is used for outdoor services during the summer.

8 Al-Aqsa Mosque

The early 8th century, El-Aqsa was razed by earthquakes and occupied by the Crusaders. It contains a *mihrab* (prayer niche) from Saladin's time and marble columns donated by Mussolini.

6 Sabil of Qaitbey

The carved stone dome of this 15th-century public fountain **(below)**, finely decorated inside and out, is unique in the Holy Land. It was built by the Mameluke Sultan Qaitbey in the shape of a tomb.

10 Qanatir

A *qanatir* (row of free-standing arches) tops each of the eight flights of steps up to the Dome of the Rock. Some of the column capitals of the arcades were reused from Roman buildings.

TOP 10 ⭐ Western Wall

Judaism's holiest place of prayer, the Western Wall or HaKotel is a huge retaining structure built by Herod the Great to hold up the Temple Mount. It is about 1,600 ft (488 m) long, but only a small section is used for prayers; most of the rest is hidden or is part of an archeological park. From 1948 to 1967, Jews were not allowed to pray at the Wall, but since its dramatic capture by Israeli paratroopers during the Six-Day War, it has once again become a place of pilgrimage.

2 Men's Section
The Wall's prayer area is divided by sex, according to Orthodox Jewish tradition, with about two-thirds of the 197-ft (60-m) stretch reserved for men. Only men are permitted to read from the Torah.

1 Prayer Notes
For centuries Jews have written prayers on slips of paper and tucked them in the crevices between the Wall's giant stones (above). Twice a year, the notes are collected and buried on the Mount of Olives.

3 Herodian-Era Stones
Limestone blocks laid on the orders of Herod – the largest weighing 520 tonnes – can be identified by their indented borders. Seven layers of stones can be seen; another 17 layers lie hidden beneath the plaza.

THE OLD CITY
The Wall is the eastern boundary of the Jewish Quarter, which was largely destroyed by the Jordanians in the 1948 war and rebuilt in 1967 after Israel's capture of East Jerusalem. North of it is the Muslim Quarter, the largest and most populous, stretching to Damascus Gate and including most of the Via Dolorosa. West of this lies the Christian Quarter, with dozens of holy places. The small Armenian Quarter is in the southwest corner, stretching to Jaffa Gate.

4 Davidson Center
Part of the Jerusalem Archeological Park, this museum holds artifacts shedding light on the city's history. There's also a virtual reconstruction of the Second Temple.

5 Chain of Generations Center
Displayed in seven rooms, glass sculptures (below) illustrate the transmission of Jewish tradition and the deep spiritual bond of Jews to Jerusalem from biblical times to the present.

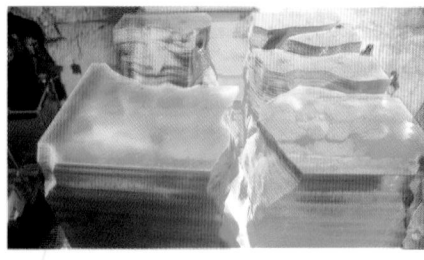

6 Robinson's Arch

Protruding from the southern end of the Western Wall, this 1st-century BC Herodian arch once held aloft a staircase leading up to the Temple Mount. Archeologists believe it was destroyed during the Roman siege of AD 70, either by attacking Roman legionnaires or besieged Jewish Zealots.

7 Southern Wall

In the late Second Temple period (including Jesus' lifetime), the broad, sloping stairway next to the Southern Wall brought worshippers through arched entrances to the Temple Mount esplanade.

8 Egalitarian Prayer Space

A section of the Western Wall below Robinson's Arch has been set aside for non-sex-segregated prayers by Jews from the Reform and Conservative movements, to which some Israelis and most Diaspora Jews belong. Many ultra-Orthodox authorities oppose this.

9 Western Wall Plaza

Jewish worshippers, some wearing the dress of the shtetl, gather at the Western Wall **(left)** to pray individually and in groups, to celebrate Shabbat, Jewish holidays and life-cycle events, as well as for swearing-in ceremonies of the IDF (Israeli Defense Forces).

10 Western Wall Tunnels

Running for over 1,315 ft (400 m) along a section of Western Wall hidden by medieval buildings, the tunnels **(above)** – and fascinating Second Temple-period arches, gates, passageways, and ritual baths – link the Western Wall Plaza with the Via Dolorosa.

NEED TO KNOW

MAP P4

Western Wall Plaza: Jewish Quarter, Old City; open 24 hrs; be prepared for airport-style security

Western Wall Heritage Foundation: english. thekotel.org

Southern Wall, Jerusalem Archeological Park, Davidson Center: open 8am–5pm Sun–Thu, 8am–2pm Fri; adm; www.archpark.org.il

Western Wall Tunnels: tours 7am–late night Sun–Thu, 7am–noon/1pm Fri; adm; reserve ahead

Chain of Generations Center: open 9:40am–11pm Sun–Thu, 7am–noon/1pm Fri; adm

- 13-year-old Jewish boys often hold bar mitzvahs here on Monday, Thursday, and Saturday mornings.

- The City of David excavations are situated just outside Dung Gate.

TOP 10 ★ Israel Museum

One of the world's leading museums of art and archaeology, the Israel Museum has a breathtaking collection representing human material culture from prehistory to 21st-century Israeli artworks. Highlights include the Dead Sea Scrolls, artifacts found at Masada, ancient Hebrew inscriptions, and centuries-old synagogues from Southern India, Northern Italy, Suriname, and Germany, plus superb works of European art, including a canvas by Rembrandt. There are also libraries, landscaped gardens, and places to eat.

1 The Shrine of the Book

Housed in the heart of the shrine are the oldest biblical manuscripts in the world: the Dead Sea Scrolls. A full-scale facsimile of the Great Isaiah Scroll – the only completely intact scroll found – forms a dramatic centerpiece **(below)**.

3 Second Temple Model

This meticulous scale model **(above)** covers almost an acre (4,000 sq m) and gives a good sense of Jerusalem's topography and architecture on the eve of the Great Jewish Revolt against the Romans (AD 66–70), a generation after Jesus' crucifixion.

4 Fine Arts Wing

The collections here include works by Cézanne, Degas, Monet, Pissarro, and Renoir, as well as Modigliani, Pollock, Rothko, and Schiele. It also has excellent exhibits of art from Asia, Africa, Oceania, and pre-Columbian America.

5 Archaeology Wing

Starting with the anthropoid sarcophagi at the entrance **(left)**, this chronological journey through the Holy Land never fails to impress. There are fine mosaic floors from Beit She'an and Nablus, as well as priceless treasures from neighboring cultures, including Egypt, Greece, and the Islamic world.

2 Ruth Youth Wing

Dedicated to interactive art activities, the Ruth Youth Wing features galleries, art and craft studios, a library of illustrated children's books, and a recycling room. Parents are encouraged to join in. The wing is most active during school vacations.

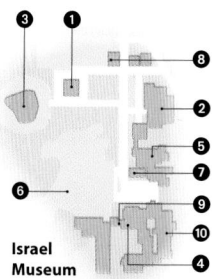

Israel Museum

7 Temporary Exhibition Galleries

These central galleries can house up to three exhibitions at a time. Past highlights have included exhibitions of Picasso's work, Yemenite silverwork, and the art of Venice's Jewish Ghetto.

DESIGN OF THE SHRINE OF THE BOOK

Inspired by the shape of the lids of the jars in which the scrolls were found, the Shrine of the Book is a landmark in architectural design. The white dome contrasts with a black basalt wall, referencing the battle between the Sons of Darkness and the Sons of Light, as described in the War Scroll. Jets of water constantly spray the dome's exterior, symbolizing the ritual purity of the desert community that wrote the Dead Sea Scrolls nearly 2,000 years ago.

6 Billy Rose Art Garden

Designed by artist Isamu Noguchi, this blends Western sculpture with elements from Japanese Zen gardens, with a Jerusalem backdrop.

8 Gift Shops

There are two stores selling high-quality gifts inspired by the museum's collections, including Judaica, jewelry, replicas, prints, and accessories.

9 Israeli Art

Exhibits here present the works of leading artists who have been active in Israel since the beginning of the 20th century, exploring their different generations and varying artistic styles.

10 Jewish Art and Life Wing

Presenting the culture and art of the Jewish diaspora from the Middle Ages to the present day, this wing (above) showcases both sacred and secular elements of Jewish civilization.

NEED TO KNOW

MAP J5 ■ 11 Ruppin Blvd, West Jerusalem ■ (02) 670 8811 ■ Egged buses 7, 9, 14, & 35; bus 100 is a park-and-ride service from Shapirim Interchange on Highway 1 to the Knesset across the street ■ www.imjnet.org.il

Open 10am–5pm Sat–Mon, Wed, & Thu; 4–9pm Tue; 10am–2pm Fri

Adm

■ Photography is not permitted in the galleries.

■ There are two routes in and out of the main galleries: one through the Route of Passage and another via the open-air Carter Promenade.

■ Mansfeld, a dairy café, has three branches with some outdoor seating. At the main entrance, Modern serves non-vegetarian fare.

Exhibits in the Israel Museum

① Herodian Royal Bathhouse (1st century BC)

This reconstructed hot room from Herod's palace at Herodion is decorated with colorful frescos, tiles, and mosaic floors. Raised on pillars and with earthenware piping built into the walls to provide heating, it was the latest in Roman technology.

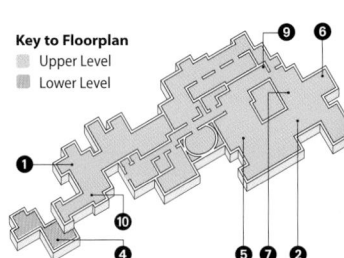

Key to Floorplan
- Upper Level
- Lower Level

Jeanne Hébuterne, Seated

② Modigliani's Jeanne Hébuterne, Seated (1918)

Amedeo Clemente Modigliani's portrait of his pregnant mistress is a classic example of his idealized style – using flowing lines to define her flat oval face, long neck, and almond eyes. When Modigliani died suddenly at the age of 36, a despairing Jeanne killed herself during her ninth month of pregnancy. Above the portrait is displayed a Congolese mask, highlighting the influence of African art on the Italian artist.

③ Kapoor's Turning the World Upside Down, Jerusalem (2010)

Anish Kapoor's stainless-steel sculpture crowns the museum's highest point. Standing 16 ft (5 m) high, its polished mirror-like surfaces capture and reverse reflections of the sky and surrounding landscape.

④ Byzantine Synagogue and Church

Early Christian and Jewish houses of prayer dating from the 4th to the 7th centuries AD are contrasted in this installation. The synagogue *bima* (chancel) is from Susiya while the church *bima* comprises marble and stone elements from 17 churches.

⑤ Leopard Head Hip Mask (17th century)

From Benin in Africa, this pendant was worn by high-ranking officials on their left hip, under a scabbard or sword. The mask is cast in brass and punched with copper studs.

⑥ Rembrandt's St. Peter in Prison (1631)

This painting of St. Peter demonstrates Rembrandt's genius for expressing spiritual qualities through the contrast of light and shadow. The saint sits in a radiant pool of light, his humanity apparent in his lined face and fisherman's hands, while large parts of the canvas remain in darkness.

Leopard Head Hip Mask

JEWISH ART AND LIFE WING

This wing comprises treasures associated with Jewish rituals around birth, marriage, and death, and ends with a stunning array of clothing and jewelry from throughout the Jewish Diaspora. The attention given to aesthetics and presentation, in addition to each object's historical value, makes an immediate impact. Particularly memorable are the two walls displaying over 100 Hanukkah lamps in lit glass cases, and the gallery of rare illuminated manuscripts that includes Maimonides' Mishne Torah from the 15th century. Visitors can follow a Synagogue Route through the reconstructed interiors of synagogues brought from Germany, Italy, India, and Suriname, each one reflecting the culture of its host country while maintaining the key features of a Jewish house of worship.

TOP 10 HIGHLIGHTS

1 20th-century wedding dress from Cochin, India

2 19th-century bridal jewelry from Izmir, Turkey

3 19th-century Hungarian funeral carriage

4 15th-century Maimonides' illuminated Mishne Torah

5 19th-century sukkah from Fishach, Germany

6 Shabbat spice boxes

7 18th-century Suriname synagogue

8 120 Hanukkah lamps

9 Esther Scrolls from Purim

10 18th- to 19th-century hooded cape from Morocco

The Vittorio Veneto synagogue (1700) from Northern Italy has been reconstructed and is part of the museum's Synagogue Route exhibit.

7 The Rothschild Room (18th century)

This Parisian salon, donated by Baron Edmond de Rothschild, is decorated with tapestries, paintings, chandeliers, and gilt paneling.

8 Turrell's Space That Sees (1992)

In the Billy Rose Art Garden, follow the gravel path down to view James Turrell's Modernist sculpture hewn from the bedrock. Looking through the white frame to a square of blue sky above feels like being inside an abstract painting. After dark, the stars provide a different perspective.

9 Rubin's The Sea of Galilee (mid-1920s)

Reuven Rubin used a naive style and clear colors inspired by Palestine's bright landscapes to capture scenes of daily life. Here he contrasts traditional and modern life, as agriculture meets nature and the Arab and Zionist worlds connect.

10 Mihrab from Isfahan (17th century)

In a mosque, the *mihrab* indicates the direction of Mecca and thus prayer. This specimen is adorned with glazed mosaics – cut from blue tiles – and Quranic verses.

Following pages Worshippers praying at Jerusalem's Western Wall

TOP 10 ⭐ Haifa

Cascading down the slopes of Mount Carmel between Haifa Bay and the Mediterranean, cosmopolitan Haifa is one of the world's loveliest port cities. The Baha'i Gardens offer stunning panoramas of the German Colony's 19th-century houses, Hadar's Bauhaus buildings, and the narrow lanes of the Arab neighborhood of Wadi Nisnas. Sprinkled throughout are excellent museums, while at the top of the hill, pine-shaded parks and upscale neighborhoods stretch along a boulevard lined with cafés and restaurants.

1 Tikotin Museum of Japanese Art

This museum puts on first-rate exhibitions of Japanese art, both traditional (including paintings, prints, ceramics, swords, and masks) and contemporary. Founded in 1959, it has won prestigious awards from the Japanese government.

2 Shrine of the Bab

One of the founders of the Baha'i faith, the Bab was executed in Iran in 1850 and reburied in Haifa in 1909. His ornate tomb, in the lower section of the Baha'i Gardens, is topped by a golden dome.

3 Hecht Museum

Hidden away on the Haifa University campus, the Hecht Museum **(left)** has a superb archeology collection, art by Manet, Pissaro, Van Gogh, and more, plus a 400 BC Mediterranean shipwreck.

Haifa

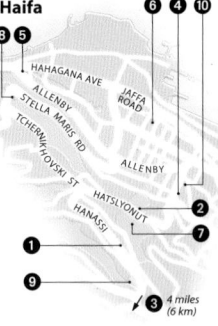

4 Beit HaGefen

Set up in 1963 to promote Arab-Jewish coexistence, this Arab-Jewish Cultural Center center organizes city walking tours, art exhibits grappling with intercultural dialogue, and the annual Jewish-Muslim-Christian Festival of Festivals.

5 Clandestine Immigration and Naval Museum

Exhibits cover the dramatic period of 1934–48, when the Zionist Movement made repeated attempts to bring Jews fleeing persecution in Europe to Palestine in defiance of the British blockade **(above)**.

6 German Colony

Established in 1868 by German Christians known as Templers, the German Colony has gone from being a prosperous village to Haifa's premier dining district.

8 Stella Maris Carmelite Monastery

Founded 900 years ago on Mount Carmel, this mountaintop monastery **(left)** has been run by the Carmelite order since the 1830s. The church is sumptuously painted.

THE BAHA'I

Founded in Iran in 1844, the Baha'i faith believes in the oneness of God and the oneness of all religions, the harmony between science and religion, and equality between women and men. Accused of heresy by Islamic authorities, its founder Baha'ullah was exiled and later jailed in Akko for the last 24 years of his life. His tomb *(see p61)* is the Baha'i faith's holiest site.

9 Gan HaEm and Zoo

Atop Mount Carmel, Gan HaEm park offers shade and a kid's playground close to the Carmel Center's cafés and shops. The adjacent zoo has been popular since 1949.

10 Wadi Nisnas

Almost unchanged since 1948, this feels more like a village than an urban neighborhood. Over 100 sculptures and installations here form part of Beit HaGefen's Museum Without Walls.

7 Baha'i Gardens

A UNESCO World Heritage Site, the Baha'i faith's world headquarters features 19 terraces of fountains and flower beds, plunging down Mount Carmel and offering breathtaking views **(above)**.

NEED TO KNOW

MAP C4

Haifa Tourist Board: 48 Ben-Gurion St; (04) 853 5606; www.visit-haifa.org

Hecht Museum: 2 HaGefen St; open 10am–4pm Sun, Mon, Wed, & Thu, 10am–7pm Tue, 10am–1pm Fri, 10am–2pm Sat; mushecht.haifa.ac.il

Tikotin Museum of Japanese Art: 89 NaNassi Blvd; open 10am–7pm Sat–Thu,10am–1pm Fri; adm; www.tmja.org.il

Zoo: 124 HaTishbi St; open Nov–Apr: 9am–4pm Sat–Thu (to 1pm Fri), May–Oct: 9am–6pm Sat–Thu (to 2pm Fri); adm; www.haifazoo.co.il

Beit HaGefen: 2 HaGefen St; open 10am–4pm Sun–Thu (to 2pm Fri & Sat); www.beit-hagefen.com

Stella Maris Carmelite Monastery: open 6:30am–12:30pm and 3–6pm daily

Baha'i Gardens: 45 Yefe Nof St; English tour noon Thu–Tue (dress modestly); www.ganbahai.org.il

Shrine of the Bab: 80 HaTzionut Ave; open 9am–noon daily (gardens until 5pm); www.ganbahai.org.il

Clandestine Immigration and Naval Museum: 204 Allenby Rd; (04) 853 6249; open 10am–4pm Sun–Thu; adm; bring your passport

■ The underground Carmelit funicular railway links the Carmel Center and Hadar with the downtown port area.

■ Eat at HaZkenim and Michel, the famous falafel rivals of Wadi Nisnas.

TOP 10 ⭐ Bethlehem

According to the Hebrew Bible, Bethlehem was the birthplace of the shepherd-boy David and the site of his coronation as the King of Israel. It is, of course, most famous as the birthplace of Jesus. In AD 326 Constantine the Great had a church built on the site, and today the Church of the Nativity is Christendom's oldest house of prayer. Just 6 miles (10 km) south of Jerusalem, Bethlehem has been under the jurisdiction of the Palestinian Authority since 1995. Once majority Christian, it is now about 75 percent Muslim.

1 Shepherds' Fields
In the nearby village of Beit Sahour lies the site where the "shepherds watched their flocks by night." Catholic and Greek churches **(above)** mark where the host of angels is believed to have appeared.

2 Banksy's Graffiti
In 2005 and 2007, the renowned UK street artist Banksy put about a dozen images on the separation wall in the West Bank. Many of his iconic artworks can be seen in Bethlehem.

3 Church of the Nativity
The cave under this church set on Manger Square has been revered as the birthplace of Christ since AD 160 – a silver star marks the spot. The church was rebuilt in 530, but many features remain from the original basilica.

NEED TO KNOW

MAP F4

Church of the Nativity: open summer: 6:30am–7:30pm daily, winter: 5am–5pm daily, closed Sun morning

Rachel's Tomb: Hebron Rd; open daily

The Milk Grotto: open 8am–5pm daily

St. Catherine's Church: open summer: 6:30am–7:30pm, winter: 5am–5pm

Baituna Al-Talhami Museum: Star St, off Pope Paul VI St; (02) 274 2589; open 8am–1pm & 2–5pm Mon–Wed, Fri, & Sat, noon–5pm Thu; adm

Palestinian Heritage Center: www.palestinian heritagecenter.com

■ Buses for Bethlehem leave from the Arab bus station located opposite the Damascus Gate in Jerusalem's Old City.

4 St. Catherine's Church

The Franciscans built this church in 1882 on the site of a 5th-century monastery associated with St. Jerome. His statue is located in the cloisters **(above)**.

5 Rachel's Tomb

The small tomb of Rachel, Jacob's wife, is always busy with women who come to pray for fertility. Cut off from Bethlehem by the separation wall, this is Judaism's third holiest site.

6 Old Market

The atmospheric souk (market) sells traditional olive-wood carvings. The Baituna Al-Talhami Museum here sells gifts and embroidery made by the Arab Women's Union.

7 Solomon's Pools

These reservoirs, 3 miles (5 km) southwest of Bethlehem, supplied water to Jerusalem from Herod's time until the 20th century. The small fort near the upper pool was built by the Ottoman Sultan Osman II in the early 17th century.

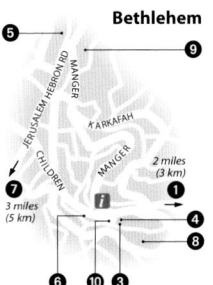

8 The Milk Grotto

Tradition has it that this cave sheltered the Holy Family **(above)** during the Massacre of the Innocents, and that a drop of Mary's milk fell here as she nursed Jesus. A chapel stands at the spot today, its walls covered with numerous testimonials to the site's power to help women conceive.

Bethlehem

(map with locations marked 1, 4, 8, 5, 9, 7, 6, 10, 3; streets labeled JERUSALEM HEBRON RD, MANGER, KARKAFAH, CHILDREN; 2 miles (3 km); 3 miles (5 km))

CHRISTMAS IN BETHLEHEM

Christmas Eve in Manger Square is an emotional experience, with Roman Catholic Midnight Mass from St. Catherine's Church being broadcast around the world. With all the denominations present in the Holy Land, Christmas celebrations stretch over a long period. Festivities can be enjoyed during the run-up, and Orthodox masses last until January 18. Details are available at the Christian Information Centre by Jerusalem's Jaffa Gate.

9 Palestinian Heritage Center

Visitors can explore a reconstructed Bedouin tent and a Palestinian living room at this center. There is a gift shop on site that sells embroidery created by local women.

10 Manger Square

Dominated by the walls of the Church of the Nativity and the 1860 Mosque of Omar, Manger Square **(below)** is the hub of the town. A Swedish-built Peace Center has visitor information.

TOP 10 ⭐ Tel Aviv-Jaffa Beachfront

Tel Aviv's glorious Mediterranean seafront stretches for 8.5 miles (14 km) from the cliffs of Herzliya to the ancient city of Jaffa. Broad expanses of sand are complemented by parks, restaurants and cafés, high-rise hotels, and a yacht harbor. Both locals and tourists flock here to swim or windsurf, sunbathe or play *matkot* (see p50), sip a cold beer or dine on schnitzel and fries, and, of course, see and be seen. The entire beachfront is paralleled by a pedestrian promenade and by part of the city's 81-mile (130-km) bike-path network.

1 Yarkon Estuary

The pedestrian-only Wauchope Bridge spans the Yarkon River right where it flows into the Mediterranean. Along both banks of the river, the walkways and bicycle paths of grassy HaYarkon Park stretch inland to playgrounds, sport facilities, and playing fields.

2 Beaches

Each of Tel Aviv's beaches **(above)** has its own personality. Metzitzim is popular with families; Hilton has separate beaches for gays, surfers, and dog owners; and Frishman and Gordon, lined with eateries, are popular with tourists. There is a gender-segregated religious beach as well.

3 Jaffa Port

According to the Bible, it was from Jaffa that Jonah set sail to meet the whale. Today, the city's picturesque port **(below)** is home to fishing craft and sight-seeing boats, while on shore the old warehouses house galleries and cultural spaces.

4 Gordon Swimming Pool

This popular saltwater Olympic-size pool is right next to the marina. Like the two children's pools, it is refilled every day with water pumped from a 492-ft (150-m) deep saline well.

THE CITY'S HISTORY

Jaffa has been a key port for thousands of years – archeologists have found fortifications dating from the 18th century BC – but neighboring Tel Aviv was founded only in 1909. The new "garden city" grew very rapidly: it was home to 2,000 residents by 1920, 34,000 by 1925, and, due to the arrival of Jewish refugees fleeing the Nazis, 150,000 by 1937. Today Tel Aviv houses over 500,000 people, including about 46,000 (two-thirds of them Arabs) in Jaffa.

Tel Aviv-Jaffa Beachfront

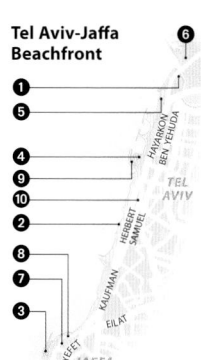

5 Tel Aviv Port

Founded in 1936, Tel Aviv's old port and seafront boardwalk are now the city's liveliest dining and nightlife area. Cafés line the cargo basin and warehouses hold shops and a food market.

6 Reading Power Station

Opened in 1938, this Modernist building is used for occasional art exhibitions. It overlooks a lovely bike path and a marble column commemorating the British assault across the Yarkon in World War I.

7 Jaffa Artists' Quarter

Destroyed by Napoleon in 1799 and rebuilt in the 1800s, Jaffa's Old City now houses the Ilana Goor Museum and artists' studios and galleries **(left)**, many hidden in the alleys between the port and the Jaffa Slope Park.

8 Jaffa Slope Park

Opened in 2010, this grassy hilltop park with its seafront promenade provides sparkling views of Tel Aviv and some much needed open space for Jaffa's historically Arab Ajami neighborhood.

9 Tel Aviv Marina

Yachts dock at Israel's oldest marina, which is also host to various sailing competitions.

10 Bauhaus Buildings

You can spot some of Tel Aviv's famous Bauhaus buildings **(above)** along HaYarkon Street, a block back from the beach. One of the finest, built in 1935, is at No. 96.

TOP 10 ⭐ Masada

In AD 72–3 at the mountaintop fortress of Masada, 967 Jewish rebels chose mass suicide over submission to Rome. Besieged by Roman legions, the rebels held out for two years before defeat became inevitable. Although there is evidence that a stronghold existed here in the 2nd century BC, it was Herod the Great who fortified the complex and added two palaces. The Romans took Masada when Herod died, but it was recaptured by the rebels during the First Jewish Revolt in AD 66. Since its rediscovery, Masada has become a symbol of the modern State of Israel.

1 The Hanging Palace

Herod's residence **(above)** was built on three tiers over the cliff's northern side. The upper level had bedrooms, and a balcony with Dead Sea views, while the lowest terrace had the royal bathhouse.

2 The Synagogue

Possibly part of the Herodian construction, this synagogue faced Jerusalem and would have served the Jewish rebels during the revolt. They built four tiers of benches along the structure's walls and added the pillars that can still be seen at the site **(below)**.

3 Sunrise

Masada opens at sunrise, when the views from the fortress over the Dead Sea all the way to the Jordanian mountains are particularly stunning.

NEED TO KNOW

MAP H5

Fortress: Off Route 90, 7.5 miles (12 km) N of Ein Bokek; (08) 658 4207; Egged bus 486 from Jerusalem; open summer: 8am–5pm Sun–Thu & Sat (to 4pm Fri), winter: 8am–4pm Sun–Thu & Sat (to 3pm Fri), Snake Path opens 1 hour before sunrise; adm; www.parks.org.il

Yigal Yadin Museum: open 8am–4pm, 1 hour later during daylight saving; adm

Sound and Light Show: (08) 995 9333; Mar–Oct: 9pm Tue & Thu; adm

▪ The Masada Visitor Center has a restaurant.

⑥ The Bathhouse
Consisting of a *caldarium* (hot room), a *tepidarium* (tepid room), and a *frigidarium* (cold room) with an immersion pool, the bathhouse was set around a large open courtyard **(left)**. The *caldarium*, with several columns supporting the raised floor, is especially well preserved.

THE SIEGE OF MASADA

First-century Jewish-Roman historian Flavius Josephus described Masada's tragic last days. After the Romans built a siege ramp and set the inner defensive walls alight, the rebels, led by Eleazar ben Ya'ir, chose death rather than surrender and slavery, killing their wives and children before taking their own lives.

⑨ Yigal Yadin Museum
This museum makes an excellent first stop as its evocative exhibits – including Roman-era jewelry, coins, footwear, and lots that may have been used in the rebels' suicide pact – provide context for the excavations atop Masada.

⑩ Water Cisterns
Of the 12 immense cisterns Herod had hewn into the mountainside, the southernmost is the largest. Rain and flood water was collected and brought up the hill to fill the cisterns on top of the rock. This system made life in Masada possible.

④ Snake Path and Cable Car
The Snake Path to the summit takes at least 45 minutes, so during the heat of the day take the cable car up **(above)**, and walk down.

⑦ Western Palace
This palace was used for ceremonial occasions and accommodating guests. Some mosaic floors and wall frescoes are superbly preserved.

⑤ Roman Ramp and Camps
On the western side is the ramp made by the Romans that enabled them to eventually break Masada's defenses. A siege wall and the camps encircling the site are still visible today.

⑧ Sound and Light Show
Twice weekly from March to October, the story of Masada's last days of resistance is told via a Sound and Light Show at the western entrance. Access is from Arad only (42 miles/68 km away).

Masada

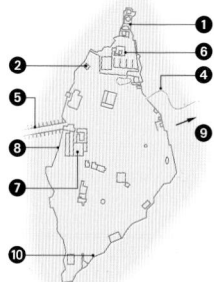

Sea of Galilee

Known as the Kinneret in Hebrew, Israel's largest freshwater lake is 13 miles (21 km) long, 8 miles (13 km) wide, and about 720 ft (220 m) below sea level. The largest town on the lakeshore is Tiberias, famed for its hot springs and tombs of illustrious rabbis. Along the perimeter are a number of important Jewish and early Christian sites associated with Jesus. In between are beaches, protected wetlands, water parks, bike paths, and hiking trails.

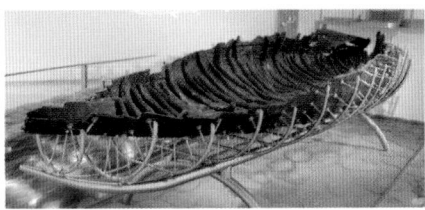

1 Kinneret Cemetery

Socialist-Zionist pioneers from the late 19th and early 20th centuries, including figures such as Berl Katznelson and the poetess Rachel, are buried in this peaceful lakeside cemetery.

2 Hamat Tiberias National Park

A gorgeous zodiac wheel mosaic in a 4th-century synagogue is the center-piece of this site, which also features hot springs and an 18th-century Turkish hammam.

3 Ancient Galilee Boat

A 27-ft (8.2-m) wooden fishing boat **(left)** that sailed the Sea of Galilee in the 1st century AD, possibly in the time of Jesus, is on display near where it was discovered in 1986, along with an explanatory movie.

4 Mount of Beatitudes

Jesus' Sermon on the Mount may have been delivered on this hillside, which has attracted Christian pilgrims since the 4th century. Today's domed chapel dates from 1938. Views of the lake, 394 ft (120 m) below, are awe-inspiring.

5 Tabgha

The Church of the Multiplication of the Loaves and Fishes **(above)** and the small Church of the Primacy of St. Peter mark the spots where Jesus is believed to have preached and performed miracles.

NEED TO KNOW

MAP B5–6, C5–6

Visitor Information: HaBanim St, Tiberias; (04) 672 5666; www.goisrael.com

Hamat Tiberias, Korazim, and Kursi national parks: open 8am–4pm Sat–Thu, to 3pm Fri (1 hr later during daylight saving), last entry 1 hr before closing; adm; www.parks.org.il

Ancient Galilee Boat: Yigal Alon Centre; open 8am–5pm daily; adm; www.bet-alon.co.il

Church of the Multiplication of the Loaves and Fishes: open 8am–5pm Mon–Fri (to 3pm Sat), Eucharist 9am Sun

Church of the Primacy of St. Peter: open 8am–5pm daily

Magdala: open 8am–6pm daily; adm; www.magdala.org

Mount of Beatitudes: open 8–11:45am, 2–4:45pm daily; parking fee

Capernaum: open 8am–5pm

Monastery of the Twelve Apostles: open 9am–5pm (to 6pm in summer)

Kinneret Cemetery: Hwy 90, 6 miles (10 km) S of Tiberias

■ The marked Shvil Sovev Kinneret trail covers 22 miles (35 km) of the lake's 37-mile (60-km) perimeter.

JESUS AT THE SEA OF GALILEE

The gospels say that Jesus spent most of his three-year ministry on the shores of the Sea of Galilee. Capernaum became his home, Mary Magdalene hailed from Magdala, many disciples came from Bethsaida in the northeast, and the lake itself is where Jesus reportedly walked on water and fed the Five Thousand. The Sermon on the Mount was delivered from a nearby hill.

⑨ Korazim National Park

Built in Talmudic times (3rd and 4th centuries AD) using local volcanic stone, Korazim is known for its synagogue and its haut-relief carvings of geometric designs, Greek-inspired figures, and floral motifs.

⑥ Kursi National Park

A 5th-century Byzantine monastery and church mark this archeological site, where tradition says that Jesus freed a man from demons by casting them into a herd of pigs (the Miracle of the Swine).

⑦ Monastery of the Twelve Apostles

At the eastern edge of ancient Capernaum, this serene Greek Orthodox complex is right on the water. The chapel, with its rich Byzantine-style art **(above)**, is topped by red domes, while peacocks parade through the delightful gardens.

Sea of Galilee

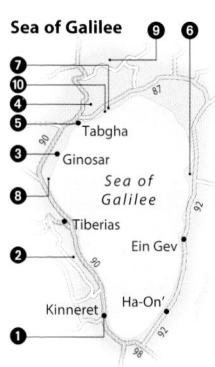

⑨ ⑥
⑦
⑩
④
⑤
Tabgha
③ • Ginosar
Sea of Galilee
⑧ • Tiberias
Ein Gev
② Ha-On'
Kinneret
①

⑧ Magdala

A copper coin minted in AD 29 was found by archeologists in Magdala's synagogue, dating the site to Jesus' time. Also here is the Magdala Stone, a rectangular block from the Second Temple period that may have been used to read the Torah.

⑩ Capernaum

Capernaum (Kfar Nahum in Hebrew), Jesus' home base during his years of ministry, is now an archeological site managed by Franciscan friars **(above)**. Highlights include a 4th-century cream limestone synagogue and a 2nd-century dark basalt synagogue.

TOP 10 ⭐ The Siq, Petra

The deep, narrow gorge known as the Siq provides a supremely dramatic entrance to Petra. All but impervious to sunlight, it twists imperceptibly downward, until suddenly it opens onto a bright square. On the other side stands the Treasury in all its glory. Since ancient times, the Siq has led traders and travelers into the heart of this Nabataean world. Modern-day explorers start in the town of Wadi Musa, from where a road leads through Bab al-Siq ("Gateway to the Siq"), a valley flanked by sandstone cliffs. In the Siq itself, the walls are pocked with votive niches, a prelude to the tombs and sculptures carved out of Petra's rock faces by the Nabataeans.

NEED TO KNOW

MAP C3 ■ 28 Wadi Musa, Jordan ■ (00962) 321 57093 ■ www. visitpetra.jo

Open summer: 6am–6pm, winter: 6am–4pm

■ Horse carriages make the 2-mile (4-km) round trip from the entrance to the Treasury along the Siq and can be arranged in advance; horses and camels are also available for short rides around the site.

■ All payments are only in Jordanian dinars; cards are not accepted.

■ Several shaded drink stands are dotted around the site.

■ Many movies, including *Indiana Jones and the Last Crusade* and *The Mummy Returns*, have been filmed at Petra.

1 Visitor Center
As well as selling entry tickets, the Visitor Center provides maps and brochures and arranges licensed tour guides in various languages. A shop at the center sells Jordanian handicrafts and gifts, some made by a local women's organization.

2 Water Channels
The Nabataeans were highly skilled hydraulic engineers, and devised sophisticated systems for water conservation and flood prevention. The Siq has two water channels that are fed by springs and supply Petra with water.

3 Obelisk Tomb
This tomb stands above the Triclinium and displays clear Egyptian influences in the four massive obelisks **(below)** that line its front.

4 Nabataean Pavements
Paving stones were laid along the Siq, probably in the 1st century AD. An extensive section can be found in the gorge near the Niche Monument.

5 Djinn Blocks

Local Arab folklore says that these 26 carved stone blocks dotted around the site **(above)** housed *djinns* (spirits), but they are probably tower tombs.

THE NABATAEANS

An ancient Arabian tribespeople, the nomadic Nabataeans (3rd century BC–1st century AD) came to control crucial desert trade routes from Arabia to Mesopotamia. Key to their success was their efficient water storage. Cisterns hidden between oases they controlled allowed them to cross the arid wilderness. Trade brought wealth, and their capital, Petra, became a center of cultural exchange.

6 View of the Treasury

As the Siq winds down to its darkest, narrowest point, a gap in the sandstone gorge suddenly unveils the rose-pink glow of the Treasury **(left)**. This first view is an awe-inspiring moment.

7 Nabataean Graffiti

Carved into the walls of the Siq, graffiti and inscriptions demonstrate the Nabataeans' literacy. Names and greetings in Latin, Greek, and Aramaic reveal their cosmopolitan society.

8 Entrance to the Siq

A monumental arch once spanned the entrance to the Siq. It collapsed in 1896, leaving only the remains of the supporting structure and pilasters carved into the rock face, best seen on the south side.

9 Niche Monument

This shrine is carved from a freestanding rock **(above)**. The central niche, bordered by columns and a frieze, holds two Djinn blocks, one with eyes and a nose.

10 Bab al-Siq Triclinium

On the south face of Bab al-Siq, this tomb exhibits the Nabataean Classical style. Like many tombs in Petra, it served as a dining chamber and was used to host feasts in honor of the dead.

The Siq, Petra

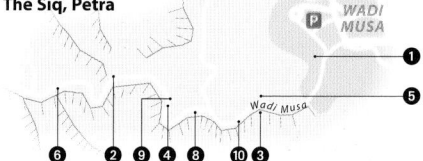

WADI MUSA

Wadi Musa

The Top 10
of Everything

**Yad Vashem, Israel's Holocaust
Museum in Jerusalem**

🔟 Moments in History

An 1842 painting by David Roberts depicting the Dome of the Rock

1 c.1800 BC: Arrival of the Hebrew Tribes

Excavations in and around Jericho show human habitation in 10,000 BC. According to the Hebrew Bible, Abraham (c.1800 BC) journeyed to Canaan and bought the Cave of the Patriarchs in Hebron. Biblical events can be corroborated with the archeological record from around King David's time (c.1000 BC).

2 586 BC: Babylonian Exile

The Babylonians conquered the Kingdom of Judea from 597 BC. The First Temple, built by Solomon, was destroyed, the Ark of the Covenant lost forever, and many Jews exiled to Babylonia.

3 AD 70: Destruction of the Second Temple

Cyrus the Great of Persia allowed the Jews to return to Jerusalem, where they built the Second Temple in the 6th century BC. Herod the Great began a reconstruction of the Temple in 22 BC, but it was destroyed by the Romans during a Jewish revolt (AD 66–70).

4 638: Arrival of Islam

Six years after Mohammad's death, Muslim armies defeated the Byzantines to conquer Jerusalem. The Dome of the Rock was built on the ruins of the Temple in AD 691. Jews and Christians were allowed to visit as pilgrims until the 10th century.

5 1099: Crusaders Capture Jerusalem

The First Crusade, launched in 1095, sought to conquer the Holy Land for Christendom. After the capture of Jerusalem in 1099, many Jewish and Muslim residents were massacred. The Muslim general Saladin (Salah al-Din) retook Jerusalem in 1187; Christian rule in the Holy Land ended with the fall of Akko (Acre) in 1291.

Painting of Crusaders in Jerusalem

6 **1516: Ottoman Rule Begins**

Ottoman Turkish rule lasted for almost exactly 400 years.

7 **1917: Balfour Declaration**

The British government declared its support for "the establishment in Palestine of a national home for the Jewish people." Ottoman rule ended when British forces captured Palestine in 1917–18.

8 **1948: Declaration of the State of Israel**

Following the 1947 decision of the UN's General Assembly to partition Palestine into two states, one Arab, the other Jewish, violence engulfed the country. Ben-Gurion's provisional Jewish government declared independence, and British forces withdrew. About 700,000 Palestinian Arabs fled or were forced from their homes.

Dome of the Rock after the Six-Day War

9 **1967: Six-Day War**

From 1949 to 1967, Jerusalem was divided along the Green Line between Israel and Jordan. The Six-Day War saw the Israelis launch a preemptive strike and capture the Golan, the Sinai, the Gaza Strip, the West Bank, and East Jerusalem.

10 **1994: Oslo Peace Process**

The 1993 Oslo Accords gave the Palestinian Authority (PA) control of West Bank and Gaza towns. In 1994 Jordan and Israel signed a historic peace treaty. Since then, Rabin's assassination, the rise of Hamas, suicide bombings, and the construction of Israeli settlements have stalled the peace process.

TOP 10 BIBLICAL AND HISTORICAL FIGURES

Palestinian leader Yasser Arafat

1 Moses (c.1250 BC)
Judaism's most important prophet led the Exodus from Egypt and received the Ten Commandments at Mount Sinai.

2 King David (c.1040–970 BC)
After capturing Jerusalem, David made it the Israelite capital of a large empire.

3 Herod the Great (c.73 BC– AD 4)
Herod was appointed King of Judea by the Romans; his great construction works are still dotted across the land.

4 Jesus (c.2 BC– AD 30)
Christians believe Jesus Christ was the Son of God, and that he died on the cross and was resurrected.

5 Rabbi Akiva (AD 40–137)
One of Judaism's greatest scholars, Rabbi Akiva was killed by the Romans for his part in the Bar Kochba Revolt.

6 Baldwin I (r.1100–18)
Crowning himself "King of Jerusalem" in the Church of the Nativity on Christmas Day, French King Baldwin was merciless to his enemies.

7 Saladin (c.1137–93)
Muslim general Salah-al Din drove the Crusaders from the Holy Land and is noted for his honor in battle.

8 David Ben-Gurion (1886–1973)
Leader of Socialist Zionism, Ben-Gurion was Israel's first prime minister.

9 Yitzhak Rabin (1922–95)
Israeli Prime Minister Rabin was assassinated by a Jewish right-wing extremist a year after winning the Nobel Peace Prize.

10 Yasser Arafat (1929–2004)
Leader of the PLO, Arafat fought for years to liberate Palestine, but was a key player in later peace negotiations.

🔟 Museums

A gallery at Yad Vashem

1 Yad Vashem, Jerusalem

MAP F4 ▪ Har Hazikaron, near Mount Herzl ▪ Open 9am–5pm Sun–Wed, to 8pm Thu & 2pm Fri ▪ www.yadvashem.org

Israel's moving memorial to the six million Jews killed in the Holocaust focuses on the victims' personal stories. The Children's Memorial is a haunting reminder of the 1.5 million Jewish children who perished, while the Garden of the Righteous Among the Nations honors non-Jews who saved Jews in Nazi-occupied lands.

2 Tower of David Museum, Jerusalem

MAP N4 ▪ Jaffa Gate, Old City ▪ Open 9am–4pm Sat–Thu, to 2pm Fri ▪ Adm ▪ www.tod.org.il

Housed in the Jerusalem Citadel, parts of which were built by Herod, this museum uses multimedia to present 4,000 years of Jerusalem's history, from the time of Canaan to the modern State of Israel.

3 Eretz Israel Museum, Tel Aviv-Jaffa

MAP X1 ▪ 2 Haim Levanon, Ramat Aviv ▪ Open 10am–4pm Mon–Wed, to 8pm Thu, 2pm Fri, & 4pm Sat ▪ Adm ▪ www.eretzmuseum.org.il

The pavilions of Eretz Israel are built around Tel Qasile, an excavated mound revealing 12 eras of human occupation. Also on view is a collection of rare glassware, some beautiful Judaica, and mosaic floors from Beit Guvrin-Maresha National Park (see p75).

4 Design Museum Holon

MAP E3 ▪ 8 Pinhas Eilon St, Holon ▪ Open 10am–6pm Tue, Thu, Sat, to 4pm Mon & Wed, & 2pm Fri ▪ Adm ▪ www.dmh.org.il

Hosting several international design exhibitions each year, this museum, designed by Ron Arad, is the pinnacle of Holon's urban-regeneration program. Five iconic rust-colored steel ribbons encircle the building. There are two galleries, a lab for interaction with design students, plus a café and shop. The museum is closed between exhibitions, so check the website before visiting.

Design Museum Holon

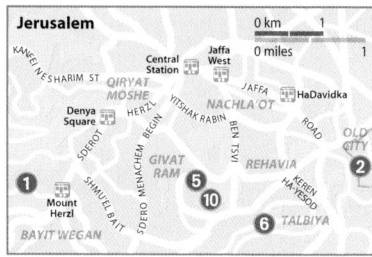

5 Bible Lands Museum, Jerusalem

MAP J5 ▪ 25 Avraham Granot St ▪ Open 9:30am–5:30pm Sun–Tue & Thu, to 9:30pm Wed, 10am–2pm Fri–Sat ▪ Adm ▪ www.blmj.org

The mutual influence of the civilizations of the ancient Near East is the focus at this superb museum, with displays of the material culture of the region.

Bible Lands Museum

6 L. A. Mayer Museum of Islamic Art, Jerusalem

MAP L6 ▪ 2 HaPalmach St ▪ Adm ▪ Open 10am–3pm Mon–Wed, to 7pm Thu, 2pm Fri–Sat ▪ www.islamicart.co.il

The scope and brilliance of Islamic civilization can be seen through illuminated manuscripts, ceramics, metalwork, and jewelry from the Arab world, Turkey, and Iran.

7 Beit HaTfutsot, Tel Aviv-Jaffa

MAP X1 ▪ University of Tel Aviv, Ramat Aviv ▪ Open 10am–7pm Sun–Wed, to 10:30pm Thu, to 3pm Sat, 9am–2pm Fri ▪ Adm ▪ www.bh.org.il

Interactive displays, dioramas, and videos reveal life in the Jewish Diaspora. Don't miss the 18 diverse models of synagogues.

8 Yitzhak Rabin Center, Tel Aviv-Jaffa

MAP W1 ▪ 14 Haim Levanon ▪ Open 9am–5pm Sun, Mon, Wed, to 7pm Tue, Thu, to 2pm Fri ▪ Adm ▪ www.rabincenter.org.il

Using state-of-the-art technology to tell the story of the birth of the State of Israel, this museum provides a compelling and relatively neutral account of the events culminating in the death of Yitzhak Rabin. The candlelit room at the end is dedicated to Rabin's memory.

9 Tel Aviv Museum of Art

MAP X2 ▪ 27 Shaul Hamelekh ▪ Open 10am–6pm Mon, Wed, Sat, to 9pm Tue, Thu, 2pm Fri ▪ Adm ▪ www.tamuseum.org.il

Israel's finest collection of art spans the 17th century to the present day, and includes works by Degas, Monet, Picasso, and Rothko. The building is an arresting geometric shape, with three of its five floors underground.

A Degas at Tel Aviv Museum of Art

10 Israel Museum, Jerusalem

Highlights of the world's largest biblical archeology collection include the Dead Sea Scrolls, a 9th-century BC inscription that mentions the "House of David," and a 6th-century BC amulet that has the Priestly Benediction on it *(see pp18–21)*.

Churches and Monasteries

Cathedral of St. James in Jerusalem

1 Cathedral of St. James, Jerusalem

MAP N5 ▪ Armenian Quarter, Old City ▪ (02) 628 2331 ▪ Open 6–7:30am & 3–3:30pm daily

This 12th-century Armenian church, redolent with incense, has an elaborate vaulted dome, gilded altars, and countless hanging oil lamps. It stands over the tomb of St. James the Apostle, whose severed head lies in the third chapel on the left. Open during services only.

2 Church of the Holy Sepulchre, Jerusalem

Different Eastern and Western Christian denominations administer various areas within the Church of the Holy Sepulchre. Don't miss the tiny Coptic chapel at the rear of the Sepulchre itself (see pp12–13).

3 Church of the Multiplication of the Loaves and Fishes, Tabgha

MAP B5 ▪ (04) 667 8100 ▪ Open 8am–5pm Mon–Fri (to 3pm Sat)

This austere Catholic church was built in the 1980s on the site of a 5th-century Byzantine chapel. It is believed to be the place where Jesus fed the 5,000 with five loaves and two fish (Matthew 15: 32–39). A mosaic in front of the altar shows a basket of bread flanked by fish (see p32).

4 Basilica of the Annunciation, Nazareth

MAP C5 ▪ Casa Nova St ▪ (04) 657 2501 ▪ Open 8am–6pm

The largest church in the Middle East, this is the traditional scene of the Annunciation. The apse of a 5th-century church encloses a sunken grotto, backed by the remains of a Crusader church. Above soars the modern edifice, consecrated in 1969.

5 Church of the Nativity, Bethlehem

This church is entered through the tiny Door of Humility, its size aimed at preventing looters from riding in on horseback. In the nave, limestone columns carry Crusader paintings of saints. Steps lead down to the Grotto of the Nativity (see pp26–7).

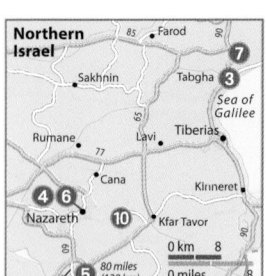

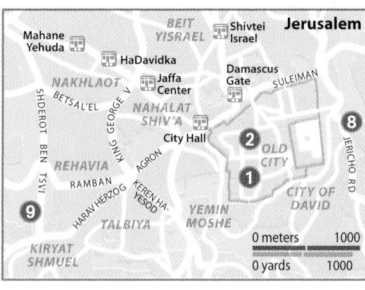

6 Centre International Marie de Nazareth, Nazareth

MAP C5 ▪ 15A Casa Nova St ▪ (04) 646 1266 ▪ Open 9:30am–noon & 2:30–5pm Mon–Sat ▪ www.cimdn.org

Opened in 2011 by a Catholic organization based in France, this elegant modern complex includes a domed chapel for prayer and meditation, a rooftop garden planted with biblical plants, a multimedia presentation on Mary of Nazareth, and, in the basement, archeological excavations from the time of Jesus.

7 Mount of Beatitudes, Sea of Galilee

MAP B5 ▪ West off Route 90 ▪ (04) 672 6712 ▪ Open 8–11:45am & 2–4:45pm daily

Overlooking the northern shore, this serene Italianate complex is believed to stand on the site where Jesus delivered his Sermon on the Mount. The domed, octagonal church from 1938 has colorful stained glass.

8 Basilica of All Nations, Jerusalem

MAP Q4 ▪ Mount of Olives, East Jerusalem ▪ (02) 626 6444 ▪ Open 8am–noon & 2–5pm daily, 1 hour later during daylight saving

Also known as the Basilica of the Agony, this Catholic church was built in 1919–24 through global donations. It stands over the rock on which Jesus is said to have prayed before his arrest. The gilded pediment mosaic depicts Christ's agony.

Monastery of the Cross, Jerusalem

9 Monastery of the Cross, Jerusalem

MAP K5 ▪ Shota Rustaveli St, West Jerusalem ▪ (052) 221 5144 ▪ Open 10am–4:30pm Mon–Sat ▪ Adm

Established in the 5th century AD, this walled, fortified monastery, just down the hill from the Knesset, was rebuilt by monks from Georgia 600 years later. Now occupied by Greek Orthodox monks, the interior has exceptional frescoes and remnants of a Byzantine mosaic.

10 Church of the Transfiguration, Lower Galilee

MAP C5 ▪ Mount Tabor ▪ (04) 662 0720 ▪ Open 8–11:45am & 2–5pm Sun–Fri

This "high mountain apart" has been identified with Christ's Transfiguration since the 4th century. Various forts and churches have stood here since, but the present Franciscan structure dates from 1924. A viewpoint offers great vistas of the Galilee.

Basilica of All Nations

TOP 10 Ancient Synagogues

Bar'am National Park's synagogue

① Bar'am National Park

MAP B5 ▪ Near Tziv'on, Hwy 899 ▪ Open 8am–4pm Sat–Thu, 8am–3pm Fri, 1 hour later during daylight saving ▪ Adm ▪ www.parks.org.il

Built in the 3rd century AD, Bar'am is one of Israel's best-preserved ancient synagogues. Made of finely carved basalt, the structure has three doorways that face south toward Jerusalem. Inside, rows of columns, some of them still in situ, held up the roof.

② Tzipori National Park

MAP C4 ▪ Off Hwy 79 ▪ Open 8am–4pm Sat–Thu, 8am–3pm Fri, 1 hour later during daylight saving ▪ Adm ▪ www.parks.org.il

An array of outstanding mosaics, including a portrait known as the "Mona Lisa of the Galilee," make Tzipori (Zippori; known as Sepphoris in Greek) one of Israel's richest Roman- and Byzantine-era sites. In the 2nd century AD, this was the seat of the Sanhedrin, the highest Jewish court. The floor of the 5th-century synagogue is adorned with Hebrew and Aramaic inscriptions and mosaics depicting a zodiac wheel and biblical scenes.

Beit Alpha mosaic

③ Umm al-Kanatir

MAP B6 ▪ Near Kibbutz Natur, Golan Heights

Jewish residents built the Golan's largest synagogue – 60 ft (18 m) long, 43 ft (13 m) wide, and 40 ft (12 m) high – in the 6th century AD, but it was turned into a rocky jumble by the great earthquake of AD 749. Archeologists are figuring out the original placement of each of piece of black basalt, and restoring the synagogue, stone by stone, to its former glory.

④ Korazim National Park

MAP B5 ▪ Near Almagor, Hwy 8277, off Route 90 ▪ (04) 693 4982 ▪ Open 8am–4pm Sat–Thu, 8am–3pm Fri, 1 hour later during daylight saving ▪ Adm ▪ www.parks.org.il

Cursed by Jesus for refusing to heed his teachings (Matthew 11:20–22), the well-preserved Mishnah- and Talmud-era village of Korazim occupies a basalt-strewn hillside overlooking the Sea of Galilee. The synagogue is decorated with fine haut-relief engravings.

⑤ Beit Alpha National Park

MAP C5–D5 ▪ Kibbutz Heftzibah 7 miles (11 km) W of Beit She'an ▪ Open 8am–4pm Sat–Thu, 8am–3pm Fri, 1 hour later during daylight saving ▪ Adm ▪ www.parks.org.il

Decorated with Israel's most renowned zodiac wheel mosaic, the floor of this Byzantine-era synagogue (5th century AD) also depicts specifically Jewish symbols, such as the seven-branched menorah, the *shofar* (ram's horn), and the Torah ark.

6 Capernaum
MAP B5 ■ Hwy 87
■ Open 8am–5pm daily

The Roman-era fishing village of Capernaum (Kfar Nahum in Hebrew) is mentioned in all four gospels. It has an impressive 4th-century synagogue, built on the foundations of a synagogue two centuries older. According to the New Testament, Jesus became angry at the people of Capernaum when they did not take his message to heart (Matthew 11:23–24).

7 Magdala
MAP B5 ■ Migdal Junction, Hwy 90 ■ Open 8am–6pm daily ■ Adm ■ www.magdala.org

The synagogue in Magdala, the birthplace of Mary Magdalene, dates from the time of Jesus' Sea of Galilee ministry. The seven-branched menorah adorning the Magdala Stone (a copy of the original that is now in Jerusalem's Israel Museum) was probably carved by an artist who had himself seen just such a menorah in the Temple in Jerusalem.

8 Shalom Al Yisrael
MAP F5 ■ Jericho, West Bank

Built in the 7th century AD, this synagogue has a mosaic floor decorated with a seven-branched menorah, a *lulav* (palm branch), a *shofar* (ram's horn), and the inscription "shalom al Yisrael" ("peace upon Israel"). Since the Oslo Accords of 1993 it has been administered by the Palestinian Authority.

9 Beit She'arim National Park
MAP C4 ■ Kiryat Tiv'on ■ Open 8am–4pm Sat–Thu, 8am–3pm Fri, 1 hour later during daylight saving ■ Adm ■ www.parks.org.il

Now a UNESCO World Heritage Site, Beit She'arim served as a hugely important centre of Jewish learning from the 2nd to 4th centuries AD. The catacombs and synagogue are decorated with geometric designs, Jewish symbols, Hellenistic motifs, and inscriptions in Hebrew, Aramaic, Greek, and Palmyrene. Yehuda HaNasi (AD 135–217), who redacted the Mishnah (the first compilation of Jewish law), lived and is buried here.

10 Katzrin
MAP B6 ■ Ancient Katzrin Park, Golan Heights ■ (04) 696 2412 ■ Open 9am–4pm Sun–Thu, 9am–2pm Fri ■ Adm ■ parkqatzrin.org.il

Known for its ornate Greek-style capitals, this black-basalt synagogue, built in stages from the late 4th to the 7th centuries AD, is surrounded by a reconstructed Talmud-era village. Hebrew and Aramaic inscriptions from 30 ancient Golan synagogues can be seen nearby in the Golan Archeological Museum.

Katzrin's black basalt synagogue

🔟 Beaches

1 Ein Bokek
MAP H5 ■ Southern Basin, Dead Sea

A room in one of the upmarket hotels here doesn't come cheap, but thanks to an Israeli law guaranteeing free public access to all beaches, floating in the mineral-rich waters here doesn't cost a shekel.

The beaches at Ein Bokek

2 Jisr az-Zarka
MAP C3 ■ Jisr az-Zarka (accessible from Hwy 4)

This lively Arab town, just north of Caesarea, has several places to eat and, a 10-minute walk away, a long sandy beach with places to change, gazebos, and lifeguards nearby.

3 Tel Aviv-Jaffa
MAP E3 ■ Tel Aviv-Jaffa

Tel Avivis looking for a break from their fast-paced lifestyle head to one of the city's 13 official beaches, each with its own personality and places to eat and drink. Stretching along 9 miles (14 km) of coastline, all have bathrooms, changing facilities, and pergolas for shade. Lifeguards are on duty May through October.

Tel Aviv-Jaffa's miles of coastline

4 Hukuk
MAP B5 ■ 2 miles (3 km) N of Kibbutz Ginosar, Sea of Galilee ■ Adm

Dozens of small beaches surround the Sea of Galilee. Some, such as Hukuk on the northwestern shore, have fine sand and facilities such as changing rooms, kids' play areas, eateries, and lifeguards, while others are just isolated strips of pebbles.

5 Herzliya Pituah
MAP E3 ■ Ramat Yam St, Herzliya, N of Tel Aviv-Jaffa

This beach town is home to many of Israel's successful tech companies and, atop a seafront cliff, some of its priciest homes. Below is a popular fine-sand beach called Arkadia. Changing facilities are available.

6 Caesarea Aqueduct
MAP D3 ■ Aqueduct St, Caesarea

To bring fresh water from Mount Carmel to Caesarea, 6 miles (10 km) to the southwest, the Romans built tunnels and aqueducts that functioned until the 12th century. Long sections of the stone-built aqueduct stand along Caesarea Aqueduct Beach. There are no facilities here.

7 Dolphin Reef
MAP D2 ■ 2.5 miles (4 km) SW of Eilat ■ Open 9am–4:30pm or 5pm daily ■ Adm ■ www.dolphinreef.co.il

Named for a pod of bottlenose dolphins that live here, this horseshoe-shaped lagoon has a sandy beach and offers the unique opportunity to swim, snorkel, and scuba dive with dolphins.

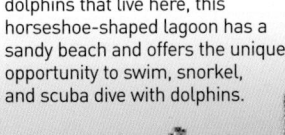

Rocky shores at Dor-HaBonim

⑧ Dor-HaBonim

MAP C3 ■ Between HaBonim and Dor, S of Haifa ■ Adm

Part of a nature reserve, this 3-mile (5-km) section of Mediterranean coast is known for its dramatic *kurkar* rock formations, tidal pools rich in marine life, tiny offshore islands, untouched beaches, and Tel Dor, the ruins of a Phoenician port town. Camping is permitted.

⑨ Beit Yanai-Michmoret

MAP D3 ■ Beit Yanai ■ Adm

Nahal Alexander, coastal Israel's most ecologically healthy river (it's a national park) flows into the Mediterranean amid pristine sand dunes dotted with grass and shrubs. Beit Yanai Beach, south of the estuary, has eateries; to the north, Michmoret Beach offers beautiful views plus beachfront restaurants. Camping is permitted.

⑩ Coral Beach

MAP D2 ■ 4 miles (7 km) SW of Eilat ■ Open 9am–5pm Sat–Thu, 9am–4pm Fri, open 1 hour later during daylight saving ■ Adm ■ www.parks.org.il

The Red Sea has some of the world's most incredible undersea life, and this marine nature reserve is the best place in Israel to experience it. The beach itself is nothing special, but get into the water and you'll discover gardens of extraordinary coral inhabited by the kind of frilly, colorful fish you can usually only see in aquariums. Snorkeling gear is available for rent.

TOP 10 SAFETY TIPS FOR THE DEAD SEA

1 Sunburn
Wear sunblock but don't stress out about sunburn – thanks to the density of the air, you'll get much less solar radiation than at sea level.

2 Dehydration
The extreme heat can cause dehydration, and so can osmosis while swimming, so drink plenty of water.

3 Salt Stings
Avoid shaving for a day or two before taking a dip – Dead Sea waters cause even the tiniest scratches to sting.

4 Eye Care
Never dunk your head below the surface – if Dead Sea water gets in your eyes, it will sting terribly.

5 Swallowing the Water
Never swallow Dead Sea water – drinking even a small quantity can be dangerous.

6 Strong Winds
Don't let the wind push you away from the coast, or you may end up floating toward Jordan.

7 Sinkholes
Watch out for sinkholes around the Dead Sea's northern basin and heed all warning signs about them.

8 Flash Floods
Rain can turn wadis in the area into dangerous torrents, so stay out of dry riverbeds if there has been rain up in the Judean Desert.

9 Rocky Seabed
Bring flip-flops, as parts of the Dead Sea have a rocky bottom.

10 Jewelry
Leave your jewelry at home – minerals in the water will discolor almost everything except 24-carat gold.

Visitor enjoying the Dead Sea

TOP 10 Children's Attractions

Bloomfield Science Museum

1 Bloomfield Science Museum, Jerusalem

MAP J4 ▪ Givat Ram, West Jerusalem ▪ www.mada.org.il

This interactive museum warrants a detour for its engaging displays on architecture, gravity, electricity, and communications.

2 Hezekiah's Tunnel, Jerusalem

MAP Q5 ▪ City of David, East Jerusalem ▪ Adm ▪ www.cityofdavid.org.il

This amazing tunnel was hacked out of the bedrock by King Hezekiah to supply water to the city of Jerusalem. Kids adore wading through the thigh-high water in the dark.

3 Mini Israel, Latrun

MAP F3 ▪ Latrun, off Rd 1 ▪ 1700 599 599 ▪ Adm ▪ www.minisrael.co.il

Tremendously enjoyable for children, Mini Israel allows them to see the country's major sights in miniature. There are about 400 scale models, some of which are dynamic.

4 Dolphin Reef, Eilat

MAP D2 ▪ South Beach ▪ (08) 630 0111 ▪ Open 9am–5pm daily ▪ Adm

Swim with a pod of bottlenose dolphins, or watch them from the floating piers. There's also a lovely beach with loungers, a restaurant, and a children's activity center.

5 Underwater Observatory Marine Park, Eilat

MAP D2 ▪ Eilat ▪ (08) 636 4200 ▪ Open 8:30am–4pm daily ▪ Adm ▪ www.coralworld.co.il

A tower that descends 40 feet (12 m) into the waters of the Gulf of Aqaba affords up-close views of the Red Sea's extraordinary corals and fish. While humans are confined to an aquarium, sea life is free to roam, gawk, and tap on the glass.

Underwater Observatory Marine Park

⑦ Rosh HaNikra Sea Grottoes, Western Galilee

MAP B4 ■ Western Galilee ■ (073) 271 0100 ■ Adm ■ www.rosh-hanikra.com

Carved out of white chalk cliffs by the pounding Mediterranean, these caves flicker with an ever-changing palette of blues. Kids love the cable-car ride, the heaving seas, and the relics of the old Haifa–Beirut railroad.

⑧ Alpaca Farm, the Negev

MAP B2 ■ Mitzpe Ramon ■ (08) 658 8047 ■ Adm ■ www.alpaca.co.il

Alpacas and llamas are reared here along with horses, camels, donkeys, and sheep. There are wool-weaving activities for kids, plus horseback riding around Makhtesh Ramon.

Alpaca Farm resident

⑨ Jerusalem Biblical Zoo

MAP F4 ■ 1 Aharon Shulov St, West Jerusalem ■ Adm ■ www.jerusalemzoo.org.il/len/

There's a special focus on species mentioned in the Bible, but you can also see red pandas, tigers, spider monkeys, elephants, and penguins at this Jerusalem zoo.

⑩ Israel Children's Museum, Holon

MAP E3 ■ 1 Mifratz Shlomo St, Peres Park ■ (03) 650 3000 ■ Call ahead to book in advance ■ www.childrensmuseum.org.il

Devoted to broadening young minds, this museum encourages interactive participation. Vision- and hearing-impaired guides conduct tours that leave a lasting impression on the museum's young visitors.

⑥ Luna Gal Water Park, Sea of Galilee

MAP B6 ■ Golan Beach ■ (04) 667 8000 ■ Open May–Sep ■ Adm

Israel's oldest water park, on the eastern edge of the Sea of Galilee, is even suitable for toddlers. Entry also allows beach access, and there are kayaks and inner tubes for hire.

🔟 **Outdoor Activities**

Camel safaris leading visitors through rugged desert landscapes

1 Skiing
www.hermonski.co.il
Snowfall can be erratic on Mount Hermon but there's usually skiing for a few weeks a year. When it's warm visitors can ride a ski lift up to the highest point in Israeli territory (7,336 ft/2,236 m) for alpine flowers and spectacular panoramas

2 Diving and Snorkeling
Dive operators: www.snuba. co.il; www.oonasdiveclub.com; www.inmodivers.de
Thanks to the Red Sea's clear water, colorful reefs, and diverse marine life, Eilat offers an excellent introduction to one of the world's most extraordinary underwater ecosystems. Operators offer scuba diving and you can rent snorkeling gear at several beaches. Or try "snuba," a cross between diving and snorkeling.

Snorkeling in the Red Sea

3 Desert Safaris
Tour operators: www.visit jordan.com, www.cameland.co.il, www.beerotayim.co.il
Some excellent outfits in the Negev offer camel trips along the Spice Route's old caravan trails. In Jordan, the striking landscapes of Wadi Rum (65 miles/105 km south of Petra), a UNESCO World Heritage Site, can be explored by camel or Jeep.

4 Water Sports
Operators: www.kiteaway.com
The Mediterranean coast is ideal for sailboarding (windsurfing), in which Israel has won three Olympic medals, and kitesurfing. Several spots near Tel Aviv and Haifa offer decent surfing, brought to Israel in the 1950s.

5 Bird-Watching
Tour operators: www.birds. org.il, www.israbirding.com, natureisrael.org/birding, www. kibbutzlotan.com, www.parks.org.il
Located on the main migration route between Africa and Europe, Israel is perfect for bird-watching. Eilat and Lotan eco-kibbutz in the Negev are good bases, as is the famed Hula Nature Reserve in the Galilee.

6 Matkot
This popular beach game uses wooden racquets and a squash ball, and only requires you to maintain the longest volley possible.

7 Rappelling and Canyoning

Tour operators: www.israel-extreme.com, www.adventure-israel.com

Also known as abseiling (*snepling* in Hebrew), rappelling down cliffs and dry waterfalls is very popular in Israel. Favorite sites include Nahal Zavitan on the Golan, Keshet Cave in the Western Galilee, and Nahal Daraja near the Dead Sea.

8 Cycling

Tour operators: www.ibike.co.il, www.abrahamtours.com, www.geofun.co.il

New trails offer ever more options for cyclists and mountain bikers, particularly in the Negev. Makhtesh Ramon has challenges for all levels and the green, hilly area of the Galilee is another top destination.

Mountain bikers on a desert ridge

9 Hiking

Tour operators: www.natureIsrael.org (SPNI), www.walkingpalestine.org

Israel boasts an extensive network of marked trails. The Society for the Protection of Nature in Israel runs guided group day hikes; seasonal trips feature migrating birds (spring and fall) and rare wild flowers (spring).

10 Horseback Riding

Tour operators: www.alpacasfarm.com, www.veredhagalil.co.il

Horseback riding is a great way to explore Israel's rural areas, as well as parts of the Mediterranean coast. There are a number of stables in the Galilee, where the rolling hills offer spectacular views.

TOP 10 HIKES

Hiking through the Red Canyon

1 Red Canyon
Off Rd 12, N of Eilat ▪ Egged bus 392
Enjoy a 1.5- to 2.5-hour trek down this colorful red sandstone canyon.

2 Mount Shlomo
Off Rd 12, N of Eilat ▪ Egged bus 392
This long hike affords terrific views from the top of the mountain over the Red Sea and Sinai region.

3 Makhtesh Ramon
Start hiking from Mitzpe Ramon to get to the crater; maps are available at the information center (see pp98–9).

4 Ein Avdat National Park
The Nahal Zin trail has some stunning pools and picnic spots (see p98).

5 Ein Gedi Nature Reserve
Most people only visit the David Falls, but if you have time, attempt the stunning Dry Canyon hike (see p97).

6 Jesus Trail
www.jesustrail.com
Walk from Nazareth to the Sea of Galilee past Tzipori and sites referred to in the New Testament.

7 Yehudiya Nature Reserve
Off Rd 87, Lower Golan ▪ www.parks.co.il
Some trails involve swimming across deep pools. Parts of the reserve may be inaccessible in winter.

8 Sea-to-Sea Hike
Three-day hike to the Sea of Galilee from the Mediterranean.

9 Israel National Trail
www.israeltrail.com
Israel's top long-distance trail runs 646 miles (1,040 km) from Kibbutz Dan, on the Lebanese border, to the Red Sea.

10 Nahal Ayun Nature Reserve
www.parks.org.il
Follow the Ayun River south from the Galilee's northernmost point, Metulla.

TOP 10 Israeli Writers

Nobel Prize winner S. Y. Agnon

world. Known for their accessibility, his enduringly popular poems have been translated into 40 languages.

① S. Y. Agnon (1888–1970)

Agnon won the 1966 Nobel Prize for Literature for works that explore the tension between modern life and Jewish tradition. Set in Eastern Europe and Palestine, they draw on traditional Jewish sources, especially the Hebrew Bible and the writings of medieval Jewish sages. His seminal novel, *The Bridal Canopy* (1931), is set in Hassidic Galicia in the early 1800s.

② Emile Habibi (1922–96)

Born in Haifa to a Christian Arab family, Habibi remained in the city after 1948, becoming a leader of the Israeli Communist Party and serving in the Knesset. His works, including *The Secret Life of Saeed: The Pessoptimist*, use satire and black humor to consider the contradictions of life as an Arab citizen of Israel.

③ Yehuda Amichai (1924–2000)

Juxtaposing colloquialisms with classical Hebrew, Amichai's poetry explores daily existence in the modern

④ Ephraim Kishon (1924–2005)

After barely surviving the Holocaust, Budapest-born Kishon moved to Israel in 1949. He began publishing in Hebrew just two years later, quickly establishing himself as a humorist and social and political satirist. Two of the movies he wrote, directed, and produced – *Sallah Shabati* (1964) and *The Policeman* (1971) – were nominated for Oscars.

⑤ Aharon Applefeld (b. 1932)

As a child, Romanian-born Applefeld escaped from a Nazi concentration camp and spent three years in hiding before moving to Palestine in 1946. His novels approach the Holocaust obliquely, with *Badenheim 1939* depicting the obliviously optimistic Jews of an Austrian spa town on the eve of World War II.

⑥ Amos Oz (b. 1939)

Born to a right-wing Jerusalem family, Israel's most widely translated author spent much of his life on socialist Kibbutz Hulda, and has long been an outspoken peace activist. His evocative novels are known for realistic characters, a lightly ironic tone, and a critical take on kibbutz life.

⑦ A. B. Yehoshua (b. 1936)

Scion of an Sephardic Jerusalem family, Yehoshua captures the mood of contemporary Israel in richly textured novels that focus on individual concerns and interpersonal dynamics. Many of his works examine the ways in which impulses and passions can strip away the veneer of civilization.

Novelist A. B. Yehoshua

8 David Grossman (b. 1954)

Jerusalem-born author and peace activist Grossman is a modernist, employing stream of consciousness, changing narrative perspectives, and a mix of realism and the fantastical. His best-known works include *The Yellow Wind* (1987), a searing nonfiction examination of Israel's West Bank occupation, and the anti-war novel *To the End of The Land* (2008), written two years after his son was killed in action in Lebanon.

Essayist and writer Etgar Keret

9 Etgar Keret (b. 1967)

Known for his inventive short story collections, essays, graphic novels, and TV and movie scripts, Keret writes about the paradoxes of life in Israel with a zany sense of humor. His short stories have appeared in *The New Yorker* and on US public radio's *This American Life* show and podcast.

10 Sayed Kashua (b. 1975)

An Israeli Palestinian who writes exclusively in Hebrew, Kashua uses tongue-in-cheek wit to portray the contradictions, ironies, and indignities of life as an assimilated Arab in Israel. His work includes three novels, a weekly newspaper column (in *Haaretz*), two TV comedy shows, and the movie *A Borrowed Identity* (2014).

TOP 10 ISRAELI MUSICIANS

1 Shoshana Damari (1923–2006)
Yemen-born singer whose husky renditions of popular Hebrew songs spanned eight decades.

2 Naomi Shemer (1930–2004)
Prolific songwriter and composer most famous for her 1967 song *Jerusalem of Gold*.

3 Arik Einstein (1939–2013)
Songwriter, singer, and actor who played a pivotal role in the development of Israeli rock.

4 Shlomo Bar (b. 1943)
Moroccan-born composer, musician, and "ethnic music" pioneer.

5 Shalom Chanoch (b. 1946)
Composer, songwriter, and singer who, in the early 1970s, was one of the founders of Israeli rock.

6 Shlomo Artzi (b. 1949)
One of Israel's most successful and beloved rock singer-songwriters and composers.

7 Yehuda Poliker (b. 1950)
Singer-songwriter whose Greek-inflected music mixes the bouzouki with the electric guitar.

8 David Broza (b. 1955)
Haifa-born singer-songwriter and virtuoso guitarist who derives his inspiration from the music of Spain, where he grew up.

9 Rita (b. 1962)
Teheran-born pop singer and actor, who sings in Hebrew and, more recently, Persian.

10 Aviv Geffen (b. 1973)
Popular rock musician, songwriter, singer, and producer, who is also a Generation X counter-culture icon.

Shoshana Damari on stage

🔟 Performing Arts

Orchestral concert performance at the Jerusalem Theatre

① Jerusalem Theatre
MAP L6 ▪ 20 David Marcus St, Talbiyeh, West Jerusalem ▪ www.jerusalem-theatre.co.il

Israel's largest cultural complex, officially the Jerusalem Centre for the Performing Arts, has four performance spaces hosting local and international dance and theater – with English surtitles for some productions – art-house films, and concerts (the Jerusalem Symphony Orchestra is based here).

Modern exterior of HaBima Theater

② HaBima Theater, Tel Aviv-Jaffa
MAP W3 ▪ 2 Tarsat Blvd ▪ www.habima.co.il

Founded in Moscow in 1917, Israel's national theater company moved to Tel Aviv in 1928. It stages modern and classic Israeli and international plays in its four auditoriums. Some productions have English surtitles.

③ Zappa Club
www.zappa-club.co.il

Israel's top sponsor of live music, Zappa hosts Israeli and international talent at venues in Tel Aviv, Herzliya, Jerusalem, Haifa, and Binyamina.

④ Cameri Theatre, Tel Aviv-Jaffa
MAP X2 ▪ 19 Shaul HaMelech Blvd ▪ www.cameri.co.il

Based in the Tel Aviv Performing Arts Center (TAPAC), the repertory company here stages Israeli plays and world classics translated into Hebrew in five auditoriums. Some productions have English surtitles.

⑤ Yiddishpiel, Tel Aviv-Jaffa
MAP W2 ▪ Performances at Tzavta, 30 Ibn Gabirol St ▪ (03) 525 4660 ▪ www.yiddishpiel.co.il.org.il

About 11 million Jews spoke Yiddish on the eve of World War II; today perhaps 600,000 do. To help keep Eastern European Jewish culture alive, Yiddishpiel stages colorful, often nostalgic, Yiddish productions.

⑥ Al-Kasaba Theatre and Cinematheque, Ramallah
MAP F4 ▪ Hospital St, Ramallah ▪ www.alkasaba.org/english.php

An active community space hosting theater productions for adults and children, and daily movies. There's also a gallery space and resto-bar.

7 Jerusalem Khan Theatre

MAP N6 ■ 2 David Remez St, West Jerusalem ■ khan.co.il

Housed in a one-time caravanserai, this atmospheric venue is home to Jerusalem's only repertory theater and hosts regular visiting companies.

8 Suzanne Dellal Centre, Tel Aviv-Jaffa

MAP U5 ■ 5 Yechieli St ■ www.bat sheva.co.il, www.suzannedellal.org.il

This is the home of the celebrated Batsheva Dance Company, founded in 1963 by Martha Graham and now led by Ohad Naharin. Housed in two beautifully renovated Ottoman-era Jewish schools, this is Israel's most important contemporary dance center.

Jerusalem's Cinematheque

9 Cinematheques

MAP N6 ■ 11 Hebron Rd, West Jerusalem; 2 Sprintzak, Tel Aviv-Jaffa ■ (02) 565 4330, (03) 606 0800 ■ www.jer-cin.org.il

Tel Aviv, Jerusalem, and Haifa have vibrant cinematheques. Jerusalem's hosts a film festival in July, screening world and new Israeli cinema.

10 Charles Bronfman Auditorium, Tel Aviv-Jaffa

MAP W3 ■ 1 Huberman St ■ (03) 621 1777 ■ www.ipo.co.il

Home to the world-renowned Israel Philharmonic Orchestra, founded in 1936 by Jewish musicians fleeing the Nazis. Its performances of Western classical music range from flagship gala series to concerts for children.

TOP 10 CULTURAL EVENTS

Tel Aviv Gay Pride parade

1 Jacob's Ladder Festival
May ■ www.jlfestival.com
A weekend of folk and world music on the shores of the Sea of Galilee.

2 International Klezmer Festival
Mid-May ■ www.klezmerim.info
Safed is the ideal venue for the world's largest festival of Jewish soul music.

3 Israel Festival
May–Jun ■ www.israel-festival.org
This is Israel's leading multidisciplinary arts festival.

4 Tel Aviv Gay Pride
Late May/early Jun
Some 200,000 revellers make this Asia's largest LGBT celebration.

5 Midburn
Mid-Jun ■ www.midburn.org
The Israeli version of Burning Man takes place in the Negev desert.

6 White Night Tel Aviv
Late Jun
Dozens of cultural events, including beach concerts and parties.

7 Karmiel Dance Festival
Mid-Aug ■ www.karmielfestival.co.il
Thousands of dancers participate in this global folk dance extravaganza.

8 Red Sea Jazz Festival
Late Aug ■ www.redseajazz.co.il
Outdoor jazz performances in Eilat by top Israeli and international talent.

9 Acco International Fringe Theater Festival
Sep or Oct ■ www.accofestival.co.il
Avant-garde theatre and street performances in Crusader-era venues.

10 International Film Festivals
www.jff.org.il, www.taufilmfest.com, www.docaviv.co.il, www.haifaff.co.il
World-class annual film festivals take place in Jerusalem, Tel Aviv, and Haifa.

🔟 Regional Dishes

A colorful spread of *meze* or *salatim* dishes at the start of a meal

1 Meze or Salatim

Most Israeli and Palestinian meals begin with a salad spread – *salatim* to Israelis or *meze* to Arabs. Hummus is, of course, the best-loved dish, but close contenders are *labane* (yogurt), *baba ghanoush* (eggplant dip), and *fattoush* (pita bread salad), while olives and pickles invariably make an appearance.

2 Falafel

The ultimate street food, falafel is delicious as well as affordable. The pita comes stuffed with tomato and cucumber salad, coleslaw, *tahini* (hummus), and a dribble of *amba* (mango chutney).

3 Sabich

Sabich Frishman: 42 Frishman St, Tel Aviv-Jaffa; Oved Sabich: 7 Sirkin St, Gavatayim

This Iraqi-Jewish pita sandwich contains potato, *tahini*, salad, spices, and parsley, but the key ingredients are fried eggplant and a hard-boiled egg. When in Tel Aviv head to Sabich Frishman, or to Gavatayim's famed Oved Sabich for a taste.

4 Shakshuka

Dr Shakshuka: 3 Beit Eshel St, Tel Aviv-Jaffa

An Israeli classic, this dish of eggs poached in a rich tomato, pepper, and onion sauce, has its roots in North Africa. Locals usually eat it for breakfast, but it is good at any time.

5 Schnitzel

Ashkenazi Jews brought the schnitzel from Austria and Germany, and it's now omnipresent. Chicken or turkey is pounded thin, coated in breadcrumbs, and pan fried. You find it in fast-food places, crammed into pita with salads, or dressed up with sesame seeds, spices, and garlic in fancy restaurants.

Falafel, a very popular street food

6 Malawach and Jahnoun

Brought to Israel by Yemenite Jews, *malawach* is a pan-fried bread served with a grated-tomato dip, hard-boiled eggs, and a spicy sauce. The same accompaniments enhance *jahnoun*, a slow-baked bread roll. Both make for a heavy meal.

7 Kibbe/Kubbe

These little croquettes are made of bulgur wheat and minced meat (usually lamb), mixed with onions and pine nuts. A staple in Iraqi-Jewish and Palestinian cuisine, they come shaped as torpedos or balls, and are sually served as *meze*.

8 Kebab and Shashlik

In the Middle East, *kebab* refers to meat (usually lamb) that has been ground and spiced, then grilled on a skewer, while *shashlik* is chunks of meat cooked the same way. Israelis grill on a *mangal* (barbeque). *Shawarma* is the local, often turkey-based, version of a gyro.

Crispy baklava on display

9 Baklava

A plate of *baklava*, in a variety of shapes and colors, is served at the end of meals across the Middle East. The layers of crisp phyllo pastry and honey-soaked chopped nuts are made even stickier by syrup. Look out for *baklava* shops in Jerusalem's Old City, Nazareth, and Haifa.

10 Knafeh

This beloved Palestinian pastry consists of gooey sweet cheese coated in crunchy pastry, drizzled with rose syrup, and cut into slices.

TOP 10 PLACES FOR HUMMUS

Bowl of chickpea hummus

1 Abu Shukri (Jerusalem)
63 Al-Wad St, Muslim Quarter
▪ Open 8am–4:30pm Mon–Fri
Known for their sour, light hummus.

2 Ta'ami (Jerusalem)
3 Shamai St, nr Zion Sq, West Jerusalem ▪ Open 9am–6pm Sun–Thu, 9am–3pm Fri
Popular for their hummus with meat.

3 Abu Hassan-Ali Karavan (Tel Aviv-Jaffa)
1 HaDolphin St ▪ Open 8am–3pm Sun–Fri
A veteran joint that some say serves Jaffa's finest hummus.

4 Abu Shaker (Haifa)
29 HaMeginim Blvd ▪ Open 8am–6pm daily
Superior hummus since 1936.

5 Ashkara (Tel Aviv-Jaffa)
45 Yirmiyahu St ▪ Open 24 hrs Sun–Thu, noon–3pm Fri
An old favorite near the Yarkon River.

6 Lina (Jerusalem)
42 Al-Khanka St, Christian Quarter
▪ Open 8am–4pm Sun–Fri, to 6pm Sat
Three generations of fine hummus.

7 Abu Suheil (Akko)
14/21 Salah al-Din St ▪ Open 8am–5pm Wed–Mon
Unpretentious, outstanding hummus.

8 Abou Maroun (Haifa)
1 Kibbutz Galuyot St, Wadi Salib
▪ Open 8am–4pm daily
This place is the pride of Haifa.

9 Sa'id (Akko)
Benjamin of Tuleda St, Market, Old City ▪ Open 6am–2:30pm Sun–Fri
Undoubtedly the best in Akko.

10 Abou Adham (Kafr Yasif)
Off Rd 70, 7 miles (11 km) NE of Akko ▪ Open 8am–5pm daily
People drive miles for this hummus.

TOP 10 Restaurants

1 Toto, Tel Aviv-Jaffa

Chef Yaron Shalev is known for intriguing, delicious, and satisfying dishes. Contrasting aromas and textures come together beautifully in calamari salad, classic tortellini filled with succulent meat, delicately seasoned fish, thin-crust pizza, and divine mille-feuille, among other dishes *(see p87)*.

2 Taizu, Tel Aviv-Jaffa

This palace of Asian-Mediterranean cuisine is known for its attention to detail, from sophisticated, palate-teasing flavors of East Asia to the ultramodern dining space. For a reasonably priced taste, drop by at midday for the business lunch menu *(see p87)*.

3 Machneyuda, Jerusalem

This restaurant cooks up Mediterranean cuisine using fresh ingredients, with the menu changing weekly depending on the season. A split-level space, it is furnished in country kitchen style, with checkered napkins on the tables, and shelves loaded with wine and various types of produce *(see p73)*.

4 Satya, Jerusalem

Satya welcomes guests with a complimentary plate of bread, olives, and other nibbles. The menu offers a wide selection of international and local classics, including seafood, many of them so attractive you might want to take a picture before digging in. It also has an excellent wine list and is open on Shabbat *(see p73)*.

Satya's olive selection

5 Fattoush, Haifa

A fixture of Haifa's German Colony culinary scene for two decades, Fattoush attracts people from all walks of life – Arabs and Jews, students and artists, locals and tourists – for Arab cuisine that is both traditional and innovative. The patio offers views of the beautiful Baha'i Gardens *(see p95)*.

6 The Norman, Tel Aviv-Jaffa

In what may be Tel Aviv's most elegant dining space, Chef Barak Aharoni blends French cuisine with English, Mediterranean, and Israeli influences. Meticulously prepared from top-quality ingredients, a meal here is an experience *(see p87)*.

The Norman, one of Tel Aviv-Jaffa's most elegant restaurants

Raphaël, Tel Aviv-Jaffa
Arguably Israel's best chef, Raphi Cohen is known for his fusion of Moroccan cooking with French techniques, creating a distinctive Mediterranean flavor. This is also the place to sample New Israeli cuisine, which uses eggplant, tomato, yogurt, *tahini*, *friki* (roasted green cracked wheat), and chickpeas *(see p87)*.

 HaBasta, Tel Aviv-Jaffa
Its location next to Tel Aviv's biggest produce market is what makes HaBasta so very Israeli and at the same time a market restaurant of the kind you might find in France. Some dishes are perennials, but others change daily based on what's available. Locals recommend trying dishes made with goat's meat and Jerusalem artichoke *(see p87)*.

Diners at Uri Buri, Akko

 Uri Buri, Akko
Facing the seaside defensive wall of Akko's Old City, Uri Buri specializes in turning the bounty of the Mediterranean into perfectly cooked, delicately seasoned dishes. Acclaimed chef Uri Yirmias is not afraid to surprise diners with unexpected combinations *(see p95)*.

Al-Reda, Nazareth
Located in the Old City, in an 18th-century mansion suffused with the élan of elite Ottoman society, Al-Reda, with its creative Levantine and Arab cuisine, has helped make Nazareth one of the most exciting culinary centers of Israel *(see p95)*.

TOP 10 WINERIES AND BREWERIES

Storage drums at Carmel Winery

1 Carmel Winery
MAP C3 ▪ Winery St, Zichron Ya'akov
Founded by Baron Rothschild in 1882. Try its Mizrachi Private Collection.

2 Golan Heights Winery
MAP B6 ▪ Katzrin, Golan Heights
Yarden is its premier label, and the Cabernet Sauvignon is highly rated. Also try the Golan and Gamla labels.

3 Margalit
MAP D3 ▪ Caesarea
Family-owned business notable for its Cabernet Franc and Enigma labels.

4 Barkan
MAP F3 ▪ Kibbutz Hulda
Famed for its Cabernet Sauvignon.

5 Clos de Gat
MAP F3 ▪ Ayalon Valley
These vineyards produce the Sycra collection, including a good Muscat.

6 Domaine du Castel
MAP F4 ▪ Ramat Raziel
Sample the good Castel Grand Vin at this family-run winery.

7 Yatir Winery
MAP H4 ▪ Arad
Yatir Forest is the flagship label of this small winery, part-owned by Carmel.

8 Adir Winery
MAP B5 ▪ Dalton Industrial Park, Upper Galilee
Award-winning wines from the Dalton Plateau area of the northern Galilee.

9 Taybeh Brewery
MAP F4 ▪ Taybeh village, near Ramallah
The only Palestinian beer, Taybeh is a golden German-style brew.

10 Golan Brewpub
MAP B6 ▪ Katzrin, Golan Heights
Four boutique beers brewed on site.

For a key to restaurant price ranges see p73

🔟 Israel and Petra for Free

1 Knesset, Jerusalem
MAP J4 ▪ Givat Ram, West Jerusalem ▪ (02) 675 3337 ▪ English tours at 8:30am, noon, 2pm Sun & Thu ▪ www.knesset.gov.il

The debating chamber, committee rooms, and artworks of Israel's 120-member parliament can be visited on an hour-long guided tour. When the Knesset is in session, visitors can also sit in on debates, (Monday and Tuesday from 4pm, Wednesday from 11am). Dress appropriately; bring your passport.

2 Supreme Court, Jerusalem
MAP J3 ▪ Givat Ram, West Jerusalem ▪ (02) 675 9612 ▪ English tours at noon Sun–Thu ▪ www.court.gov.il

Filled with architectural references to over two millennia of construction in the land of Israel, the home of Israel's Supreme Court elegantly combines enclosed and open-air spaces. Opened in 1992, it is acclaimed as one of Israel's most magnificent public buildings.

3 Baha'i Gardens, Haifa
Cascading down the slopes of Mount Carmel, the exquisitely landscaped Baha'i Gardens (see pp24–5) bring together flowers, manicured grass, burbling streams, dramatic formal staircases, and fabulous views of the Mediterranean. The layout was inspired in part by traditional Persian gardens. The gold-domed Shrine of the Bab is surrounded by the lower gardens.

Ma'agan Michael Ship, Hecht Museum

4 Hecht Museum, Haifa
One of Israel's best archeology collections brings alive the cultures of the Levant from the time of Canaan to the Byzantine period. The star exhibit is the Ma'agan Michael Ship, which plied the Mediterranean 2,500 years ago (see p25).

5 Rosh Pina, Upper Galilee
MAP B5 ▪ HaHalutzim St, Rosh Pina

Much as they were in the 1880s, the quiet lanes of Rosh Pina's old town are lined with stone houses. Visit the old synagogue, a small museum, the Baron's Garden, and the cemetery.

6 Ramat HaNadiv, Zichron Ya'akov
MAP C3 ▪ Zichron Ya'akov ▪ (04) 629 8111 ▪ Open 8am–4pm Sat–Thu, to 2pm Fri ▪ www.ramat-hanadiv.org.il

Near the southern end of Mount Carmel, this beautiful hilltop park was built as a memorial to Baron Edmond de Rothschild. Trails lead through landscaped gardens to fine views of the Mediterranean.

Baha'i Gardens, Haifa

7 Old City, Akko (Acre)

Inhabited for at least 4,000 years, the mixed Jewish-Arab port city of Akko (see p93) is surrounded by massive walls. Many of the Old City's famous Crusader sites charge entrance fees, but visitors can explore the ramparts, sea wall, the souk (market), and the four *khans* (caravanserais) for free.

8 Yad Vashem, Jerusalem

On a forested hillside at the western edge of Jerusalem, the Yad Vashem complex (see p40) is Israel's official Holocaust memorial. The History Museum commemorates Jewish victims of Nazism through their possessions and the testimony of survivors, while the Art Museum displays works created in hiding in ghettos and concentration camps.

Yad Vashem's Hall of Names

9 Ein Bokek, Dead Sea

MAP H5 ▪ Ein Bokek

The same Dead Sea beaches enjoyed by luxury hotel guests are, by law, open to the public for free. A seaside promenade links the beaches with changing rooms and other facilities.

10 Baha'i Gardens and Shrine of Baha'ullah, near Akko

MAP B4 ▪ 3 miles (5 km) NE of Akko's Old City, near Bustan HaGalil ▪ Open 9am–4pm daily except Baha'i hols, inner garden and shrine 9am–noon Fri–Mon ▪ www.ganbahai.org.il

The burial place of Baha'ullah, the founder of the Baha'i faith, is surrounded by serene, formal "paradise gardens." This holy site is a place of pilgrimage. Dress modestly.

TOP 10 BUDGET TIPS

Jerusalem's light rail (tram)

1 For cash advances, use a credit/debit card that offers a low (or zero) foreign and cash transaction fee and a good exchange rate. Check all fees with your card provider before traveling.

2 To get to and from Ben Gurion Airport, take the train rather than a taxi. If traveling between Jerusalem and the airport, take the train, Afikim bus 485, or a shared Nesher taxi.

3 Take public transportation, including trains, *sherut* minibuses, and – using a rechargeable Rav-Kav smart card – urban and intercity buses.

4 If you rent a car, get insurance through your credit card (check coverage and get a letter from your issuer before you leave home).

5 Explore Tel Aviv-Jaffa by renting one of the 2,000 green city-owned Tel-OE-Fun bicycles available at 200 stations (www.tel-o-fun.co.il).

6 Head to the beach on foot or by bicycle – at almost all beaches, the only fee is for parking.

7 Save on accommodation costs by sleeping in a dorm bed at the 30-plus affiliates of Israel Hostels (www.hostels-israel.com).

8 Fill up on local healthy, delicious street food, such as falafel, sabich, and hummus.

9 Shop for picnics at markets such as Mahane Yehuda in Jerusalem and Shuk HaCarmel in Tel Aviv-Jaffa.

10 If you plan on visiting several nature reserves and national parks, buy a Green Card, valid for 14 days.

Religious Holidays and Festivals

Holy Saturday celebrations at the Church of the Holy Sepulchre, Jerusalem

1 Purim
Late Feb/Mar

This festival commemorates the deliverance of the Jews of ancient Persia from annihilation. The Book of Esther is read in synagogues, children dress up, and parades are held in some cities, including Holon.

2 Passover (Pesach)
Late Mar/Apr

Passover, or Pesach, remembers the liberation of the Jews from captivity, and their Exodus from Egypt. During the week-long festival, Jews eat symbolic foods, including *matzah* (unleavened bread). The first and last days are official public holidays.

3 Easter
Mar/Apr/May

Celebrated on different dates by the Eastern and Western churches, Easter is a movable feast. On Good Friday and Easter Sunday, the Via Dolorosa is a sight to behold. Most magnificent is the Holy Saturday celebration in the Church of the Holy Sepulchre *(see pp12–13)*.

4 Eid al-Fitr
Mar/Apr/May/Jun

The three-day Muslim festival of Eid al-Fitr marks the end of Ramadan, the month of fasting. It is celebrated with communal prayers, giving new clothes and gifts to children, and spending time with family.

5 Eid al-Adha
May/Jun/Jul/Aug

Eid al-Adha honors Ibrahim's (Abraham's) willingness to sacrifice his son to God. It also marks the end of the *Haj* (pilgrimage) to Mecca. The four-day event involves prayers, feasts, and charitable donation.

6 New Year
Sep/Oct

Rosh HaShanah, the Jewish New Year, marks the start of ten days

Passover at Jerusalem's Western Wall

of prayer. The Muslim New Year begins on the first day of Muharram. January 1 is not a public holiday.

 Yom Kippur
Sep/Oct

The Day of Atonement, marking the end of the ten days of penitence that begin on Rosh HaShanah, is Judaism's most solemn day. Many Jews fast from sundown to sundown. In Jewish areas no one drives, and pedestrians and cyclists take over.

 Sukkot
Late Sep/Oct

Beginning five days after Yom Kippur, this joyous seven-day holiday honors both the fall harvest and the 40 years the Children of Israel spent in the desert after the Exodus. Observant Jews erect a *sukkah* (temporary shelter) on rooftops and balconies.

A *sukkah* built on a balcony

 Hanukkah
Late Dec

The Jewish Festival of Lights commemorates the re-consecration of the Temple in Jerusalem during the Maccabean Revolt (167–160 BC), and lasts eight days. Each night, families light a *hannukiya* (candelabrum), one candle on the first night, two on the second, and so on.

 Christmas
Dec/Jan

Western and Eastern churches celebrate Christmas at different times. Each denomination also has its own traditions of prayer services and processions. On December 24, Jerusalem's Latin Patriarch leads a procession to Bethlehem.

TOP 10 RELIGIOUS FAITHS

1 Judaism
The oldest Abrahamic religion is based on a covenantal relationship between God and the Jewish people.

2 Samaritans
A dissident sect of Judaism, Samaritans live either in Nablus or Holon and now number just over 700.

3 Karaites
A subsect of Judaism dating back to the 8th century, Karaites believe that only the written Torah is binding. About 40,000 live in Israel.

4 Orthodox Christianity
Greeks are the dominant Orthodox group in Jerusalem. Russians, Ethiopians, and Armenians also have a presence.

5 Catholicism
The Latin church arrived in Jerusalem with the Crusaders.

6 Islam
Founded by the Prophet Mohammad, Islam conquered the Holy Land six years after his death in 638 AD.

7 Druze
The Druze split from Islam in the 11th century; a central tenet is the "oneness of God." About 120,000 live in Israel.

8 Circassian
Fleeing Russian persecution in the Caucasus, this Sunni Muslim group arrived in Ottoman Palestine in the late 1800s. They live in two Galilee villages.

9 Ahmadiyya
A revivalist Islamic sect founded in 1889, who believe that Mirza Ghulam Ahmad is the Messiah.

10 Baha'i
The Baha'i believe in the unity of all religions. The sect is based in Haifa, while its holiest site is in Akko.

Orthodox church, Jerusalem

Israel and Petra
Area by Area

Colorful boats moored in
Akko's Old City harbor

TOP10 Jerusalem

This ancient city is sacred to the three great monotheistic faiths. Crammed with churches, mosques, synagogues, museums,  and archeological sites, the Old City has a chaotic romance that takes the breath away. Palestinian-majority East Jerusalem contains fascinating sights and good nightlife, while the Jewish city hosts excellent museums, markets, and restaurants. Jerusalem's 3,000-year history has been turbulent, to say the least. From 1949 to 1967, the city was divided along the Green Line, with Jordan controlling the east, including the Old City. The 1967 war saw Israel take control of the entire city. The mix of cultures and religions jostling against each other here leaves a lasting impression.

Church of All Nations mosaic, Mount of Olives

JERUSALEM

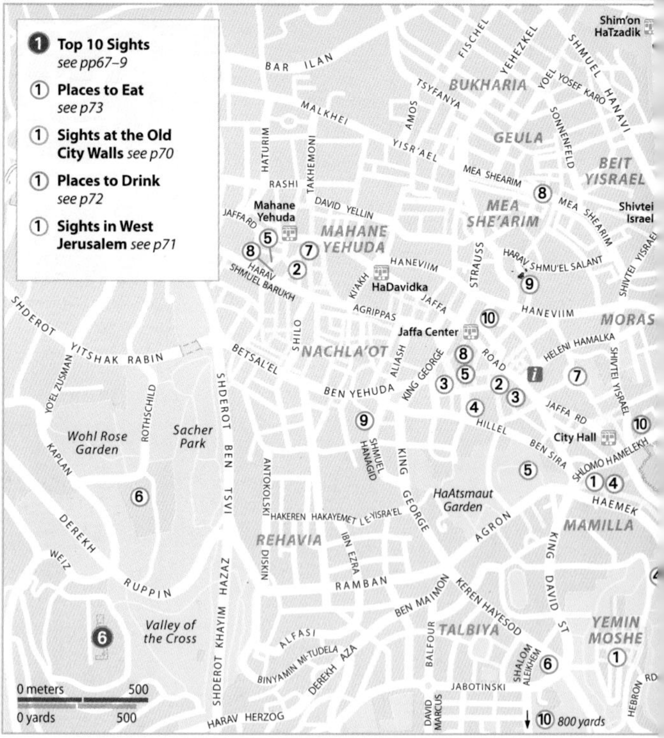

- **1** Top 10 Sights
  see pp67–9
- **1** Places to Eat
  see p73
- **1** Sights at the Old City Walls see p70
- **1** Places to Drink
  see p72
- **1** Sights in West Jerusalem see p71

0 meters 500
0 yards 500

↓ **10** 800 yards

Ramparts and courtyards, the Citadel

1 The Citadel

**MAP N4 ■ Jaffa Gate, Old City
■ Open 9am–4pm Sat–Thu, 9am–2pm
Fri ■ Adm ■ www.tod.org.il**

This imposing fortress, also known
as the Tower of David, dominates
Jaffa Gate. King Herod built three
towers here in the 1st century BC

(the stones from this period have
recessed frames), but most of the
present-day complex is from the
14th and 16th centuries. Inside, the
Tower of David Museum illustrates
the history of Jerusalem. There are
also great viewpoints (including the
ramparts) and a courtyard garden.

2 Temple Mount

Map Q4

Known to Muslims as Al-Haram
ash-Sharif (the Noble Sanctuary),
the Temple Mount is where
Abraham offered his son as a
sacrifice to God, according to both
Jewish and Muslim traditions. Site
of the ancient Jewish Temples, the
modern-day Mount is graced by the
Dome of the Rock, Al-Aqsa Mosque,
and other Islamic structures.

3 Jerusalem Archaeological Park

**MAP P5 ■ Inside Dung Gate ■ (02) 627
7550 ■ Open 8am–5pm Sun–Thu, 8am–
2pm Fri ■ Adm ■ www.archpark.org.il**

This site reveals Jerusalem's history,
from the First Temple period to the
Umayyad era. Start with the displays
of findings at the Davidson Center.
Key remains include the vestiges of
Robinson's Arch, a Herodian shopping street, a medieval tower, and
Umayyad palaces. The stairs on the
south side once led up to the Second
Temple. At the bottom of the steps
are *mikvehs* (ritual baths), where
pilgrims first purified themselves.

Jerusalem Archaeological Park

4 Church of the Holy Sepulchre

This most important of churches is tucked away amid a warren of shops in the Christian Quarter. To the right of the door, steps lead up to the Chapels of the Franks. This was the Crusaders' ceremonial entrance to Golgotha, sealed by the Muslims after they re-took the city in 1187. The last five Stations of the Cross are within the church. Four are in Golgotha; the last is Jesus' tomb itself *(see pp12–13)*.

Dome, Church of the Holy Sepulchre

Objects are beautifully presented, with excellent background information. For a peaceful interlude, wander among the sculptures of the Billy Rose Art Garden *(see pp18–21)*.

7 Walls and Gates

MAP P4 ■ Ramparts Walk: 9am–5pm Sat–Thu (till 4pm winter), 9am–2pm Fri (only the southern ramparts are open on Fri); Adm

Seven gates, dating mostly from the time of Suleyman the Magnificent, pierce the city walls. Jaffa Gate is L-shaped to slow down attackers. The most impressive is Damascus Gate, with crenellated battlements above and the remains of the original gate and plaza below. There are lion emblems on each side of Lions' Gate. The smallest is Dung Gate, close to the Western Wall; Zion Gate is bullet-scarred from 1948. The Old City Ramparts Walk affords astonishing views in all directions.

> **NAVIGATING THE OLD CITY**
>
> At Jaffa Gate the Citadel will be on your right, the Christian Quarter on your left. Straight ahead are the souks leading to the Muslim Quarter and, eventually, to the Via Dolorosa and Damascus Gate. From the Citadel, turn right and you'll come to the Armenian Quarter and, following the ramparts, Zion Gate, the Jewish Quarter, and the Western Wall.

5 Western Wall

Worshippers come day and night to Judaism's holiest site; non-Jews can also leave prayers here. The huge stone blocks were part of the Temple Mount's retaining wall. A tour follows the eerie Western Wall Tunnel to finally emerge on the Via Dolorosa *(see pp16–17)*.

6 Israel Museum

Israel's national museum, opened in 1965, houses a magnificent collection of archaeology, Jewish ritual objects, art, and design.

8 Mount of Olives

MAP Q4, R4, R5 ■ Old City ■ Hours vary, but everything is open Tue and Thu mornings

Rising over the eastern edge of the Old City and famed for its ancient Jewish cemeteries and views of Temple Mount, this hill is venerated by Christians as the site of Gethsemane, where Jesus prayed before his betrayal, and of his Ascension. Here the 1924 Basilica of All Nations (Basilica of the Agony) is adorned with

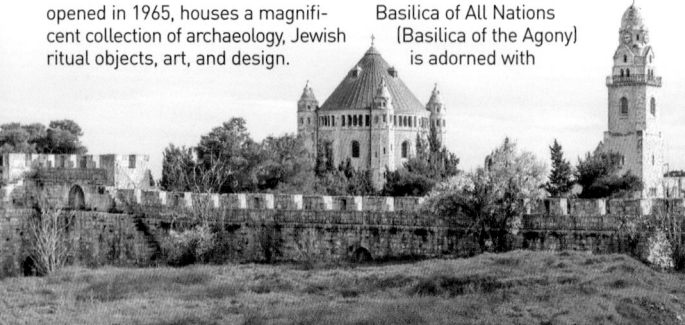

glittering mosaics, while the Church of Mary Magdalene (1888) has seven onion-shaped domes. Hidden among the trees are other churches linked to the last events of Jesus' life.

9 Old City Souks
MAP P4

The souks are the most instantly captivating part of the city. Leading down from Jaffa Gate, David Street is lined with souvenirs shops selling everything from Israeli army caps and Palestinian *kaffiyeh* to Nativity scenes. A metal staircase leads to the rooftops. David Street continues into Chain Street, where stalls merge into fabulous Mamluk buildings.

Colorful stalls in the Old City Souks

10 Mount Zion
MAP N5 ■ Dormition Abbey: open 9am–noon & 12:30–5:30pm Mon–Sat, 10:30–11:45am & 12:15–5:30pm Sun ■ Hall of the Last Supper: open 9am–5pm

This ancient site has significant biblical associations. A Crusader-era hall is believed to be the site of Christ's Last Supper, with the Tomb of David located directly below. Dormition Abbey, with its conical dome and tall bell tower, is venerated as the place where the Virgin Mary fell into "eternal sleep."

Mount Zion

VIA DOLOROSA

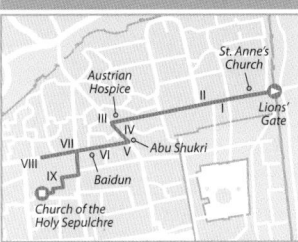

MORNING

Millions believe that the Via Dolorosa (Way of Sorrows) was the last path Jesus walked, on the way to his crucifixion. From the spot at which he was condemned to the place where he was crucified, Stations of the Cross mark each event. Start at Lions' Gate and check out the acoustics in **St. Anne's Church**. A little way ahead is the First Station, outside Al-Omariyya Boys School. Opposite, the **Monastery of the Flagellation** is the Second Station. Keep walking, under the Ecce Homo Arch, to the T-junction with Al-Wad Street. The Third Station is on your left, and to the right is the **Austrian Hospice** café (see p72). Stop here for a coffee. The Fourth Station is at the Armenian Church. Have lunch at **Abu Shukri** (see p57), slightly farther on to the left.

AFTERNOON

Turn right and find the Fifth Station of the Cross and the ascent to Golgotha. Shortly after the Sixth Station, the **Baidun** shops (28 Via Dolorosa, (02) 626 1469) are worth a visit. The Via Dolorosa meets souk Khan al-Zeit, where you'll find the Seventh Station. A short way up El-Khankah Street is the Eighth. Return to Al-Zeit, turn right and right again, and continue on to the doorway of the **Ethiopian Monastery** (see p12), where a Roman pillar marks the Ninth Station. Steps lead through the chapel to the Parvis in front of the **Church of the Holy Sepulchre**. The final five Stations are inside.

See map on pp66–7

Sights at the Old City Walls

1 Muristan
MAP P4

Originally the site of an 8th-century pilgrim hospice, Muristan has one of city's oldest churches, St. John the Baptist, and close by, the Lutheran Church of the Redeemer, whose bell tower offers amazing views.

2 The Cardo
MAP P4

In Byzantine times, this was the city's main thoroughfare. Excavations and reconstructions have turned it into an exclusive shopping arcade.

3 Lady Tunshuq's Palace
MAP P4 ■ El-Takiya St

The Mamluks' distinctive *ablaq* technique – using bands of alternate colored stone – can be seen here. The three soaring doorways are inlaid with marble, and there is stalactite decoration on the windows.

4 City of David
MAP Q5 ■ Maalot Ir David

Believed by archeologists to be the location of King David's capital, this site has turned up finds that include houses from as far back as the 10th century BC. Don't miss the tour of Hezekiah's Tunnel *(see p48)*.

5 Convent of the Sisters of Zion
MAP P3 ■ Via Dolorosa

Situated below Ecce Homo Arch, this convent contains the Struthion Pool and the flagstone *"lithostratos."*

6 Garden Tomb
MAP P3 ■ Conrad Schick St

Some believe this – and not the Church of the Holy Sepulchre – to be the site of Jesus' crucifixion. The garden is an island of serenity.

7 Rockefeller Museum
MAP Q3 ■ 27 Sultan Suleiman St ■ (02) 628 2251

Built in the 1930s and managed by the Israel Museum, this archeology museum has Crusader-era marble lintels from the Church of the Holy Sepulchre, 8th-century beams from Al-Aqsa, and stucco figurines from Hisham's Palace in Jericho *(see p76)*.

8 Zedekiah's Cave
MAP P3 ■ (02) 627 7550

Zedekiah is said to have escaped from the Babylonians in 586 BC via this massive cave. Herod also quarried it for building materials.

9 Hurva Square
MAP P5

This square is dominated by the rebuilt Neo-Byzantine Hurva Synagogue. An adjacent minaret is all that remains of the 14th-century Mosque of Sidna Omar.

10 Valley of Jehoshaphat
MAP Q4

This valley, where it is believed that the dead will be resurrected on the Day of Judgment, contains the so-called Tomb of Zechariah, with a pyramidal roof, and the conically roofed Absalom's Tomb.

Valley of Jehoshaphat

Sights in West Jerusalem

1 Yemin Moshe
MAP N5

The highlight of this small area of delightfully renovated flower-filled lanes is Mishkenot Shaananim, which was built in the 1850s as a communal housing block but now functions as an artists' guesthouse.

2 Mahane Yehuda and Nachla'ot
MAP L2 & L3 ▪ **Off Agrippas St**

For over 100 years Mahane Yehuda has been a buzzing market; now its restaurant scene and nightlife is burgeoning too – bars and cafés replace the market stalls at night. Nearby, the alleys of Nachla'ot are worth exploring.

3 Nachalat Shiv'a
MAP M3

This old neighborhood has great bars and restaurants, plus arty shops along its main alleyway. To the north lie Zion Square and Ben Yehuda Street – full of cafés and college kids.

4 U. Nahon Museum of Italian Jewish Art
MAP M3 ▪ **27 Hillel St** ▪ **(02) 624 1610**

This museum contains a synagogue from the Veneto, complete with lavish gilded Baroque stucco. Also on display are silver Torah finials and illuminated manuscripts, and an ancient wooden Ark from Mantua (1543).

5 Mamilla
MAP M4

The 1949–67 armistice line ran between Mamilla and the walls of the Old City. Some of the original 19th-century buildings have been incorporated into an upscale shopping mall.

6 Givat Ram
MAP J4

This hilltop neighborhood is home to the Knesset, the Supreme Court, and government ministries, as well as the Israel and Bible Lands museums, and a campus of the Hebrew University.

Holy Trinity Church, Russian Compound

7 Russian Compound
MAP M3

Built for Russian pilgrims in the 1860s, this enclosure's huge edifices include Sergei's Courtyard, the Church of the Holy Trinity, and a half-quarried monolithic column.

8 Mea She'arim
MAP M2

This enclave of ultra-Orthodox Jews, planned by German architect Conrad Schick (1822–1901), resembles an 18th-century Polish ghetto. Ashkenazi food, black suits, and children abound. Dress modestly when visiting.

9 Ethiopia Street
MAP M3

This charming lane houses the circular Ethiopian church, designed by Conrad Schick, and a 19th-century Arab mansion at No. 6a.

10 German Colony
Emek Refaim St

Along this fashionable street, cafés, bars, and shops occupy 19th-century Templer buildings and old Arab houses. A farmers' and craft market is held on Fridays.

See map on pp66–7

Places to Drink

1 Jerusalem Hotel
MAP N2 ■ Nablus Rd, East Jerusalem ■ (02) 628 3282 ■ Closed 10:30am–12:30pm

Enjoy draught Taybeh in this crowded vine-covered courtyard. Western and Middle Eastern food is served.

2 Austrian Hospice
MAP P4 ■ 37 Via Dolorosa, Old City ■ (02) 626 5800 ■ Open 10am–10pm

This garden café is a joy. A limited drinks menu keeps things simple.

Café at the Austrian Hospice

3 Barood
MAP M3 ■ Feingold Courtyard, 31 Jaffa Rd, West Jerusalem ■ (02) 625 9081 ■ Open 12:30pm–1am Mon–Sat

This atmospheric bar-restaurant in a pretty courtyard is a great spot for a beer, and also serves Jerusalem-style Sephardic dishes. Superb selection of spirits and liqueurs, too.

4 Mamilla Hotel
MAP M5 ■ 11 King Solomon St, West Jerusalem ■ (02) 548 2222 ■ Rooftop: open 6pm–midnight Sun–Thu, noon–11pm Fri & Sat; Mirror Bar: open 8pm–late Sun–Thu, 9:30pm–late Sat

The modern rooftop bar at the Mamilla Hotel has plush, lounge-style seating. The Mirror Bar boasts trendy lighting, a cocktail bar, and excellent DJs.

5 Birman
MAP M3 ■ 8 Dorot Rishonim, West Jerusalem ■ (02) 623 6115 ■ Open 7pm–2am daily

Birman offers live music with an emphasis on jazz, along with a well-stocked bar and fusion bar food.

6 Borderline
MAP P1 ■ 13 Shimon HaTzadik St, East Jerusalem ■ (02) 532 8342 ■ Open noon–2am daily

This expat haunt has a popular garden patio and is open till late.

7 Casino de Paris
MAP L2 ■ 3 Mahane Yeduda St, West Jerusalem ■ (02) 650 4235 ■ Open noon–late

Well hidden in the Georgian Market, this bar is named after a Mandate-era British officers' club. Great tapas.

8 Bolinat
MAP M3 ■ 6 Dorot Rishonim, just off Zion Sq, West Jerusalem ■ (02) 624 9733 ■ Open 24 hours

In the heart of the New City, this café-bar-restaurant serves light Italian-style salads and sandwiches. Hosts event nights and is popular with a young crowd.

9 American Colony
MAP P1 ■ 1 Louis Vincent St, off Nablus Rd, East Jerusalem ■ (02) 627 9777 ■ Cellar Bar opens 6pm

Mingle with journalists, intellectuals, and artists over a drink here. The cave-like Cellar Bar is open all year.

10 Notre Dame Center
MAP N4 ■ 3 HaTsanhanim, opposite New Gate, West Jerusalem ■ (02) 627 9177 ■ Open 5pm–1am Mon–Thu, noon–1am Fri–Sun

Indulge in a glass of wine and a platter of Continental cheese while admiring the splendid views from the center's rooftop restaurant.

Places to Eat

1 Rooftop
MAP N4 ▪ 1 King Solomon St, Mamilla, West Jerusalem ▪ (02) 548 223 ▪ Closed lunch Sun–Thu ▪ $$$
This Italian-style brasserie offers panoramic Old City views alongside meat, fish, pasta, and salad dishes made with top-quality ingredients.

2 Tmol Shilshom
MAP M3 ▪ 5 Yoel Moshe Salomon St ▪ (02) 623 2758 ▪ Open 8:30am–11:30pm Sun–Thu, to 2:30pm Fri, 8–11:30pm Sat ▪ $$
Dine on tasty vegetarian and fish dishes, surrounded by books. Situated in a 19th-century stone house, tucked away off a courtyard.

3 Arabesque
MAP P1 ▪ American Colony Hotel, 1 Louis Vincent St, East Jerusalem ▪ (02) 627 9777 ▪ Open 11:30am–6pm & 7–10:30pm ▪ $$$
The Middle Eastern and international menu is good, but it is the atmosphere that draws guests.

Gracious interiors of Arabesque

4 The Eucalyptus
MAP N5 ▪ 14 Khativat Yerushalayim St, Hutzot HaYotzer, West Jerusalem ▪ (02) 624 4331 ▪ Closed lunch, Fri ▪ $$$
Set in a beautiful stone courtyard, this is famed for food inspired by scenes from the Bible.

PRICE CATEGORIES
For a three-course meal for one with half a bottle of wine (or equivalent meal), taxes, and extra charges.
....
$ under $25 $$ $25–55 $$$ over $55

5 Machneyuda
MAP K2 ▪ 10 Beit Yaakov, Mahane Yehuda ▪ (02) 533 3442 ▪ $$
Fresh meat, fish, and vegetarian dishes are complemented by a great cocktail and wine list.

6 Satya
MAP M5 ▪ 36 Keren HaYesod St, Rehavia, West Jerusalem ▪ (02) 650 6808 ▪ Closed lunch Sun–Fri ▪ $$$
Intimate, stylish restaurant serving Mediterranean fish, seafood, and meat sourced from local markets.

7 Askadinya
MAP P1 ▪ 11 Shimon HaTzadik St, Sheikh Jarrah, East Jerusalem ▪ (02) 532 4590 ▪ Open 24 hours ▪ $$$
Set within an atmospheric Ottoman mansion, Askadinya offers Middle Eastern and international dishes.

8 Sima
MAP L2 ▪ 82 Agrippas St, West Jerusalem ▪ (02) 623 3002 ▪ Closed Fri eve, Sat until sunset ▪ $$
Jerusalem's best-known Middle Eastern grill and steakhouse. Start with the kubbeh soups.

9 Mona
MAP L4 ▪ 12 Schmuel HaNagid St, West Jerusalem ▪ (02) 622 2283 ▪ Closed lunch Sun–Thu ▪ $$$
High-quality Mediterranean seafood, meat, and vegetarian dishes.

10 Anna Italian Cafe
MAP M3 ▪ 10 HaRav Agan St, West Jerusalem ▪ (02) 543 4144 ▪ Close Fri eve, Sat until sunset ▪ $$
Modern Italian, from handmade pasta to pizza and fish, served under vaulted ceilings or on the patio of the historic Ticho House. Vegetarian dishes too.

See map on pp66–7

TOP 10 Around Jerusalem

Interior of the Ibrahimi Mosque, Hebron

Several full- or half-day excursions can be made from Jerusalem. Destinations to the west are in Israeli territory; those to the north, east, and south are in the West Bank. Travel between the two is relatively simple. Remote monastic communities located in stunning settings in the southern Judaean Hills are worth a visit, while the northern hills are speckled with pale stone walls and olive orchards. Here, Nablus exudes charm, while Ramallah is a lively city for nightlife. One of Israel's most impressive vistas is to be found at Herodion, near Bethlehem, and the oasis city of Jericho has a sultry vibe all its own.

AROUND JERUSALEM

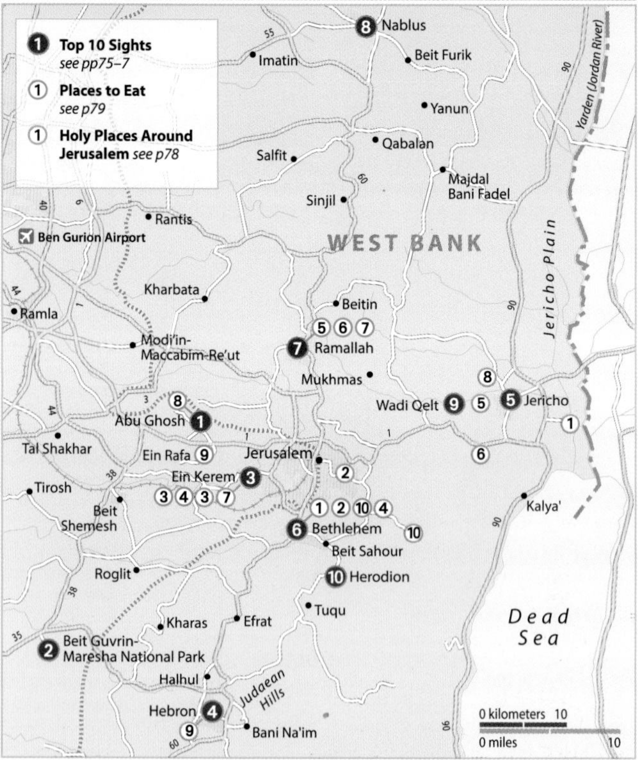

- **1** Top 10 Sights
  see pp75–7
- **1** Places to Eat
  see p79
- **1** Holy Places Around
  Jerusalem see p78

8 Nablus
Imatin • Beit Furik
• Yanun
• Qabalan
Salfit • Majdal Bani Fadel
Sinjil •
• Rantis
Ben Gurion Airport
WEST BANK
Kharbata
• Ramla
Modi'in-Maccabim-Re'ut
• Beitin
5 **6** **7**
7 Ramallah
Mukhmas • **8**
Wadi Qelt **9** **5** **5** Jericho **1**
8 Abu Ghosh **1**
Tal Shakhar
Ein Rafa **9** Jerusalem **2** **6**
Tirosh • Ein Kerem **3**
3 **4** **3** **7**
Beit Shemesh **1** **2** **10** **4**
6 Bethlehem **10** Kalya'
• Beit Sahour
Roglit • **10** Herodion
Kharas • Efrat • Tuqu
2 Beit Guvrin-Maresha National Park
Halhul • Judaean Hills
Hebron **4**
9 • Bani Na'im

Jericho Plain

Yarden (Jordan River)

Dead Sea

0 kilometers 10
0 miles 10

1 Abu Ghosh

MAP F4 ■ **10 miles (16 km) W of Jerusalem** ■ **Superbus 185** ■ **Crusader Church: open 8:30–11am & 2:30–7pm Mon–Wed, Fri, & Sun; Notre Dame de l'Arche de l'Alliance: open 8:30–11:30am & 2:30–5pm**

The Crusaders believed this now Israeli-Arab village to be Emmaus, where Christ appeared after his resurrection, and so the Knights Hospitallers built a Romanesque church here in the 12th century – it still stands, almost unchanged. On top of the hill is the Church of Notre Dame de l'Arche de l'Alliance, built in 1924 over a Byzantine church.

Russian Monastery, Ein Kerem

2 Beit Guvrin-Maresha National Park

MAP G3 ■ **Off Route 35, 33 miles (53 km) SW of Jerusalem** ■ **www. parks.org.il**

This undulating park is riddled with a network of caves. Quarried since Phoenician times, it has small surface holes revealing spiral staircases, water cisterns, burial chambers, and columbaria. The ancient Judaean city of Tel Maresha is little more than a mound, but the burial caves of its Sidonian citizens bear painted friezes depicting hunters and musicians. The apse of the Crusader Church of St. Anne is striking, while the Bell Caves are carved with Christian and Arabic inscriptions. The remains of a Roman amphitheater can be seen opposite the park entrance.

3 Ein Kerem

MAP F4 ■ **4 miles (7 km) W of Jerusalem** ■ **Light Rail, then Egged bus 28 from Har Herzl**

Tradition holds that Ein Kerem was the home of John the Baptist. Churches commemorating his life dot the village, the most striking being the Russian Monastery with its golden onion domes. Artisans' studios are sprinkled around the village and the surrounding hills make for pleasant walking. This is the perfect place to visit on Shabbat, when the churches remain open.

4 Hebron

MAP G4 ■ **25 miles (40 km) S of Jerusalem, West Bank** ■ **Egged bus 160**

Political tension is ever present in this populous town, divided between an Arab majority and hardcore Jewish settlers. Most areas are controlled by the Palestinian Authority and international peacekeepers; others are patrolled by the Israeli military. The Cave of Machpelah/Ibrahimi Mosque is split between the two religions (see p78). The Arab markets and old souk offer respite and a chance to buy the famed local glassware.

Caves, Beit Guvrin-Maresha National Park

5 Jericho

MAP F5 ■ 25 miles (40 km) E of Jerusalem, West Bank ■ Arab bus 36 to Al-Azariyya, then service taxi ■ Tel Jericho and Hisham's Palace: open 8am–6pm Sat–Thu, 8am–5pm Fri (closes 1 hour earlier in winter) ■ Adm

Settled 10,000 years ago, Jericho is reputedly the world's oldest continuously inhabited city. The Book of Joshua describes how the Israelites brought down Jericho's walls with a trumpet blast, and excavations at Tel Jericho have uncovered the remains of 7,000-year-old walls and a stone tower. A cable car connects the Tel to the Monastery of the Temptation on the cliff face *(see p78)*. Hisham's Palace, built in 724, lies in ruins, but retains its mosaic floors.

6 Bethlehem

Revered as the birthplace of Jesus, the imposing Church of the Nativity in Manger Square is the most important sight in Bethlehem. There is also an attractive Franciscan church and a Greek Orthodox site with Byzantine remains. The town center, with its narrow lanes, exudes an old-world charm *(see pp26–7)*.

Church of the Nativity, Bethlehem

TRAVELING IN THE WEST BANK

Although tourists are almost never a target, it is wise to stay informed about the security situation. Organised tours are still available, but you should take care when traveling anywhere in the West Bank and avoid all large gatherings. Due to restrictions on travel, consular assistance may be limited in this area.

Cable cars at the ancient city of Jericho

7 Ramallah

MAP F4 ■ 10 miles (16 km) N of Jerusalem, West Bank ■ Arab bus 18 ■ Tourist Information Center: Issa Ziadeh St; (02) 294 5555 ext 123; Open 9am–5pm Sat–Thu

This city at the heart of Palestine has tons of atmosphere. Al-Manarah Square is the commercial center, chock-full of vendors, shoppers, and noise. The Old City retains its Ottoman charm, and the mausoleum of Yasser Arafat in Al-Bireh is worth a visit. Weina Ramallah Festival, held in July, is a window into Palestinian culture. Ramallah is also known for its nightspots.

8 Nablus

MAP E4 ■ N of Jerusalem, West Bank ■ Arab bus 18 to Ramallah, then service taxi

A maze of souks, cobbled streets, and crumbling mansions, Nablus is an antidote to modern life. Believed by some Jews to be the site of Joseph's Tomb, the area remains a political hot spot. An Ottoman clock tower, Turkish hammams, and Roman amphitheaters are dotted around town. Nearby Mount Gerizim is home to the Samaritans *(see p63)*.

9 Wadi Qelt

MAP F5 ■ West Bank, signed off Route 1

This stunning 17-mile (27-km) ravine between Jerusalem and Jericho has a path along its full length, lined with

A WALK IN EIN KEREM

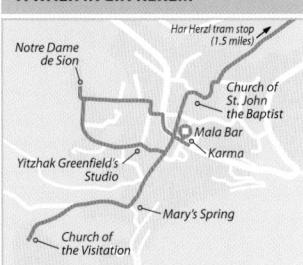

Har Herzl tram stop (1.5 miles)

Notre Dame de Sion

Church of St. John the Baptist

Mala Bar

Karma

Yitzhak Greenfield's Studio

Mary's Spring

Church of the Visitation

▶ **AFTERNOON**

After lunch, take the Light Rail to Har Herzl. Disembark, follow the sign to Yad Vashem down a side road, then turn immediately left into the forest, where a stony track descends through a wooded valley. This agreeable walk finishes less than 30 minutes later in Ein Kerem, at the rear of the Catholic **Church of St. John the Baptist** (see p78). The church opens at 2:30pm, so if you're early, stop to have coffee and snack at one of several hole-in-the-wall cafés.

After visiting the church, cross the main road and follow the sign to Mary's Spring, which is topped by a quaint mosque. From here, steps ascend to the right, to the **Church of the Visitation** (see p78). Admire the split-level church and great view, and then retrace your steps. Before the main road, turn left and follow the sign to painter Yitzhak Greenfield's studio to see his Jerusalem-inspired work. Continue to the Notre Dame de Sion Guesthouse (closed on Sunday) and ring the bell to enter. You can visit the church and cemetery, and sit a while in the peaceful garden, which has wonderful views across the valley to the golden domes of the Russian Monastery. The lane loops back to the main road. There is no shortage of restaurants and café-bars to choose from, but a failsafe option for dining is **Karma** (see p79), which has plenty of window seating. Afterwards, enjoy a beer at **Mala Bar** (see p79), which outdoor heating on chilly evenings.

palm trees. A Herodian aqueduct also follows the course of the stream. The hike passes St. George's Monastery (see p78) and continues to Jericho. The Roman road along the top of the gorge is accessible by car.

10 Herodion

MAP F4 ▪ Route 356, 7 miles (11 km) SE of Bethlehem, West Bank ▪ Taxi from Bethlehem ▪ Open summer: 8am–5pm Sat–Thu, 8am–3pm Fri; winter: 8am–4pm Sat–Thu

This magnificent hilltop palace is named after Herod the Great, and ruins of bathhouses, towers, and mosaics from his time are dotted around the site, along with his tomb. The cone-shaped summit affords amazing views, and below lie pools and gardens from Herod's day, plus churches added by Byzantine rulers.

Reconstructed tomb, Herodion

See map on p74

Holy Places Around Jerusalem

1 Monastery of St. Gerasimos

MAP F5 ■ Route 90, SE of Jericho

This complex was founded by St. Gerasimos in the 5th century. Nearby, Qasr al-Yehud may have been where John baptized Jesus.

2 Bethany

MAP R5 ■ Al-Azariyya village, E of Jerusalem

This tranquil cluster of buildings marks where Jesus is believed to have raised Lazarus from the dead. There's a Franciscan church, Lazarus' Tomb, a silver-domed Greek church, and a mosque here.

3 Church of St. John the Baptist

MAP F4 ■ Ein Kerem

This 17th-century Franciscan church was built over the ruins of Byzantine and Crusader structures. Steps lead down to the Grotto of St. John.

4 Church of the Nativity

The traditional site of Jesus' birth has been commemorated by a church since the early 3rd century. Deep inside the church, the precise spot is marked by a 14-pointed silver star (see p26).

5 St. George's Monastery

MAP F5 ■ Off Route 1, 17 miles (27 km) NE of Jerusalem, Judean Hills

This 5th-century Greek monastery is hewn into the side of a stunning gorge, Wadi Qelt.

6 Nebi Musa

MAP F5 ■ Off Route 1, 6 miles (10 km) S of Jericho, Judean Hills

Sultan Baybars built a shrine to Moses here in 1269. The cenotaph is now revered by Muslims as Moses' tomb.

7 Church of the Visitation

MAP F4 ■ Ein Kerem

Designed by the Franciscan monk Antonio Barluzzi, this two-tiered church commemorates Mary's visit to the mother of John the Baptist.

8 Monastery of the Temptation

MAP F5 ■ 1 mile (2 km) N of Tel Jericho

This cliffside Greek monastery was built around the grotto where the Devil is said to have tempted Jesus.

9 Cave of the Patriarchs

MAP G4 ■ Hebron, 25 miles (40 km) S of Jerusalem

Revered by Jews as the Cave of Machpelah and by Muslims as the Ibrahimi Mosque, this perennially tense Herodian complex – with a mosque and a synagogue – is the second holiest Holy Land site for both religions.

10 Mar Saba Monastery

MAP F5 ■ Off Route 398, 11 miles (17 km) E of Bethlehem, Judean Hills

This remote desert retreat was founded in AD 482 by St. Saba, whose remains are said to be inside the church. Women cannot enter the monastery.

Church of the Nativity

Places to Eat

PRICE CATEGORIES

For a three-course meal for one with half a bottle of wine (or equivalent meal), taxes, and extra charges

$ under $25 $$ $25–55 $$$ over $55

① Riwaq Restaurant and Coffee Shop, Bethlehem

MAP F4 ▪ Jerusalem–Hebron Rd ▪ (02) 276 6777 ▪ Open 8am–11pm daily ▪ $$

Located in the atmospheric Jacir Palace hotel, Riwaq offers Levantine specialties, salads, and cocktails.

② Dar al-Balad, Bethlehem

MAP F4 ▪ Main St, Beit Sahour ▪ (02) 274 4007 ▪ Open 10am–11pm ▪ $

Set in a restored old house in the center of Beit Sahour, Dar al-Balad serves Palestinian dishes and salads.

③ Karma, Ein Kerem

MAP F4 ▪ 74 Ein Kerem St, Ein Kerem ▪ (02) 643 6643 ▪ Open 10am–midnight Sun–Wed, 10am–1am Thu–Sat ▪ $$

The extensive menu at this split-level place includes salad, pizza, pasta, and steak in generous portions.

④ Mala Bar, Ein Kerem

MAP F4 ▪ 76 Ein Kerem St, Ein Kerem ▪ (02) 642 2120 ▪ Open 6pm–late Sun–Thu, noon–late Fri, 10am–late Sat ▪ $$$

Salads, sandwiches, pasta, and meat dishes are served at this cute candlelit restaurant-bar, which has tables along the village's main street. There are heaters in winter and a cozy indoor space to huddle up in.

⑤ Pronto's Resto-Café, Ramallah

MAP F4 ▪ Al-Rahsheed St ▪ (02) 298 7312 ▪ Open 8am–midnight ▪ $$

Cozy trattoria with the best pizza in town. Artifacts decorate the warm-colored walls, and the front patio is a great spot for a draft Taybeh.

⑥ Ziryab, Ramallah

MAP F4 ▪ Salah Building, Rakob (Main) St ▪ (02) 295 9093 ▪ Open 11am–late daily ▪ $$

A spacious café with tasty Eastern and Western food, as well as alcohol.

⑦ Azure, Ramallah

MAP F4 ▪ 35 al-Ma'ahed St ▪ (02) 295 7850 ▪ Open 11am–midnight daily ▪ $$

This old converted villa has a smart restaurant, a large bar, and a popular garden patio. The burgers are legendary; the menu also includes Arab and Asian food. Cocktails available.

Seating at Azure's bar area

⑧ Lebanese Restaurant, Abu Ghosh

MAP F4 ▪ 88 HaShalom St, Abu Ghosh ▪ (02) 570 2397 ▪ Open 8am–11pm ▪ $

Heaven for hummus-lovers. Main dishes include Middle Eastern grills.

⑨ Majda, Ein Rafa

MAP F4 ▪ Ein Rafa, off Route 1, opposite Abu Ghosh ▪ (02) 579 7108 ▪ Open 6–11pm Thu, 9am–9pm Fri, 10am–4pm Sat ▪ $$

Run by an Arab-Jewish couple, Majda mixes Levantine cooking with New Israeli cuisine.

⑩ Afteem, Bethlehem

MAP F4 ▪ Manger Sq ▪ Open 8am–late Mon–Sat ▪ $

Near the Church of the Nativity, this is fabulous for falafel and hummus.

See map on p74

🔟 Tel Aviv-Jaffa

Greek image, Jaffa Visitor Centre

Founded in 1909 by 66 families, Tel Aviv (Hill of the Spring) has come far in little over a century. The modern face of Israel, the city is a center for contemporary thought, cuisine, nightlife, and culture. Designed as a garden city in 1925, it is characterized by lovely parks, palm trees, and wide boulevards. Countless cafés and restaurant-bars line its streets, and the Mediterranean beach adds to the atmosphere. From the 1930s to the 1950s, Jewish architects fleeing Germany designed 4,000 Bauhaus buildings here, leading UNESCO to declare the "White City" a World Heritage Site in 2003.

TEL AVIV-JAFFA

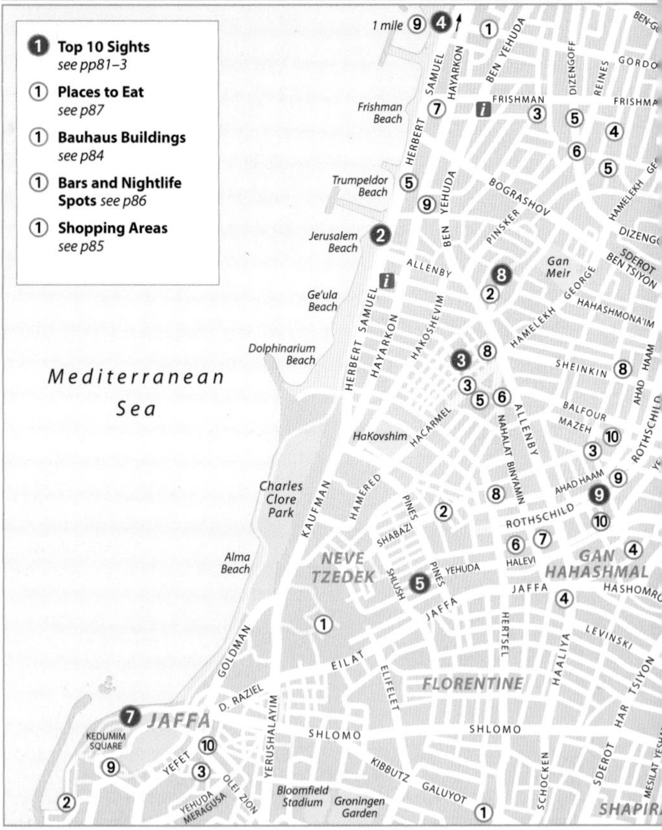

- **1** Top 10 Sights *see pp81–3*
- ① Places to Eat *see p87*
- ① Bauhaus Buildings *see p84*
- ① Bars and Nightlife Spots *see p86*
- ① Shopping Areas *see p85*

Mediterranean Sea

1 Ramat Aviv
MAP X1 ▪ Palmach Museum: 10 Chaim Levanon; (03) 643 6393; call ahead; www.palmach.org.il

An upmarket suburb, Ramat Aviv is home to Tel Aviv University, whose grounds house the excellent Beit HaTfutsot (Museum of the Jewish People) (see p41). Among other interesting museums along the southern edge are the Eretz Israel Museum and the Yitzhak Rabin Center (see p41). Between them sits the Palmach Museum, telling the story of the Jewish guerilla fighters who took on the British and the Arabs after World War II.

2 Beachfront Promenade
MAP U2

This is the youthful soul of Tel Aviv-Jaffa. Stretching along the city's edge, the beaches are popular all year long, especially in summer, when people come to sunbathe and play *matkot* (see p50). Weekends are liveliest, especially after dark when the beachfront bars start buzzing. The southern end has the best surfing, but swimmers should take note of the flags – the currents are strong.

Yemenite Quarter's HaCarmel Market

3 Yemenite Quarter
MAP V3

Bang in the city center, the Yemenite Quarter is a warren of tiny streets of low-rise, shabby-chic houses, dotted with hole-in-the-wall eateries. It merges into the HaCarmel Market (see p85), the city's largest fresh food market. Pedestrianized Nahalat Binyamin Street's eclectic buildings blend Moorish, Classical, and Art Nouveau styles (see p85).

4 Tel Aviv Port
MAP E3 ▪ Farmers' Market: Open 8:30am–8pm Mon–Sat ▪ www.namal.co.il

The city's revived port (*namal*) has undulating stretches of wooden decking and a Mediterranean vibe. Restaurants, cafés, and shops line the boardwalk. Great for families during the day, it is the perfect place for an evening drink; later it's a busy nightlife spot. In Hangar 12, an eco-building powered by green energy, there is a farmers' organic market.

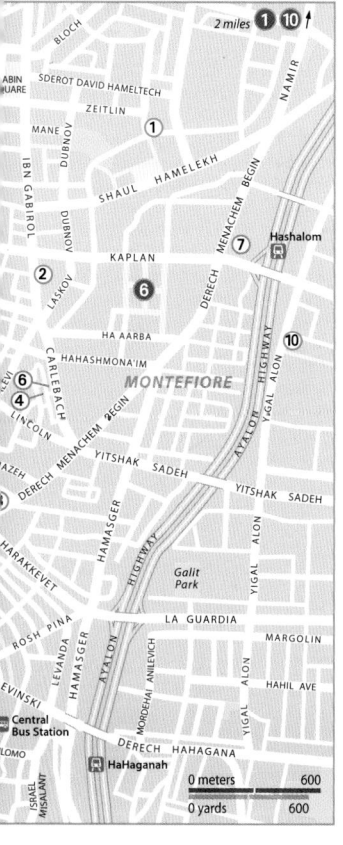

Charming Neve Tzedek Street

⑤ Neve Tzedek
MAP U4 ■ Gutman Museum of Art: 21 Shimon Rockach St; (03) 516 1970; open 10am–4pm Mon–Thu, 10am–2pm Fri, 10am–3pm Sat ■ Adm

Built in the 1880s as the first Jewish neighborhood of Jaffa, Neve Tzedek boasts flower-filled lanes, boutiques, and places to dine. Its focal point is the Suzanne Dellal Centre (see p55), which hosts cultural events. Nearby, a museum dedicated to Israeli artist Nachum Gutman displays his paintings of the new city. To the south, the trendy bohemian neighborhood of Florentine is undergoing transformation and is also worth a visit.

BAUHAUS

Also known as International Style, Bauhaus architecture is easy to spot: clean-lined, unornamented buildings with horizontal ribbon windows, vertical "thermometer windows" that supply light to stairwells, and elongated balconies with rounded corners.

---

⑥ Sarona Market
MAP X3 ■ www.saronamarket.co.il/en

A more upmarket adaptation of the HaCarmel Market (see p85) or Jerusalem's Mahane Yehuda (see p71), this indoor market is a delight for foodies. Sarona was a German Templer colony built in the 19th century, and you can now stroll among the restored houses adjacent to the north of the market before eating at one of the many restaurants.

⑦ Jaffa
MAP T6 ■ Jaffa Visitor Center: Kedumim Square, Old Jaffa; (03) 5184015; www.goisrael.com ■ Most businesses stay open on Shabbat

Located just south of Tel Aviv, this ancient port (see pp28–9), long home to both Arabs and Jews, was ransacked by Napoleon in 1799 but subsequently rebuilt. The main square is marked by an Ottoman clock tower (1906). Roman columns from Caesarea and Ashkelon were used to build the Mahmoudiya Mosque (1812), which also has a Suleyman fountain. Gan HaPisga, a hilltop park, affords dazzling views of the waterfront, especially at night. Jaffa is also a great place to shop, with its flourishing artists' quarter and flea market (see p85).

⑧ Bialik Street
MAP V3 ■ Beit Ha'ir: 27 Bialik St; (03) 724 0311; open 9am–5pm Mon–Thu (till 8pm Tue), 10am–2pm Fri & Sat; www.beithair.org

Many historic buildings line this peaceful street. Beit Ha'ir, the old town hall, is now a museum telling Tel Aviv-Jaffa's history. The eye-catching building next door is the Felicja Blumental Music Center, which hosts classical music concerts. Opposite, the Design Museum of the International School has furniture and pieces of European Bauhaus design. The house of Chaim Bialik at No. 22 has been restored with original furnishings and decor. A few doors down, the Reuven Rubin Museum has a display of his paintings, and a preserved studio.

9 Rothschild Boulevard

MAP W3 ■ Independence Hall:
(03) 517 3942; open 9am–5pm Sun–
Thu, 9am–2pm Fri; adm ■ Haganah
Museum: (03) 560 8624; open
8am–4pm Sun–Thu; adm

One of the city's most prestigious
addresses, this leafy street is lined
with some fine Bauhaus architecture
(see p84). Independence Hall, at No.
16, was the home of Meir Dizengoff,
the city's first mayor, and where Ben-
Gurion declared Israel's independence on May 14, 1948. At No. 23,
the Haganah Museum documents
the origins of the IDF.

Interior of Independence Hall

10 HaYarkon Park

MAP E3

Running along the Yarkon River in the
north of the city, this park has a kids'
adventure playground, a bird park,
and tropical garden. Row boats
can be rented on the lake, and the
Sportech complex has a climbing
wall, basketball courts, and a skate
park. On the northern edge is Luna
Park, complete with a roller coaster;
east is the Meymadion Water Park.

Boats, HaYarkon Park lake

A DAY DOWN THE PROMENADE

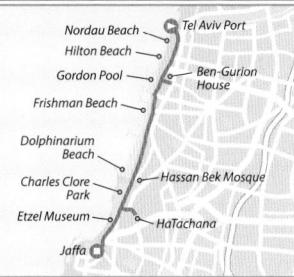

Tel Aviv Port
Nordau Beach
Hilton Beach
Gordon Pool
Ben-Gurion House
Frishman Beach
Dolphinarium Beach
Charles Clore Park
Hassan Bek Mosque
Etzel Museum
HaTachana
Jaffa

▶ MORNING

The 3.5-mile (5.5-km) promenade
is an enjoyable walk (to avoid the
worst of the heat, this itinerary
can be started in the mid-
afternoon). Bring your towel and
sunblock, and pick your favorite
beach. First, try a refreshing
organic juice at the farmers'
market at **Tel Aviv Port**. Heading
south, you'll pass walled Nordau
Beach, gender-segregated by day
for Orthodox Jewish bathers. Next
is the Hilton Beach, set below
Independence Park and a lively
and gay-friendly spot. The south
side of the beach is one of the
best spots for surfing. Continue
to the marina, bobbing with small
yachts, where anyone can use the
famous Gordon Pool ($13–19).
Make a quick detour inland to
No. 17 Ben-Gurion Street and
check out Ben-Gurion House.
Come back to Gordon Beach and
have a coffee or a beer at the
excellent **Gordo Beachfront Café**.

AFTERNOON

Further on, Frishman Beach
attracts large crowds. Stick to the
promenade until you reach the
Hassan Bek Mosque in **Manshiye**.
Tel Aviv-Jaffa's hippies congre-
gate on adjacent Dolphinarium
Beach on Friday afternoons for
drumming, capoeira, and jug-
gling. **Charles Clore Park** contains the Etzel Museum. Head
inland to trendy **HaTachana** *(see
p85)* for tapas at the Vicki Cristina
wine bar or browse the shops.
Head back to the promenade
and you're almost in **Jaffa**.

See map on pp80–81 ←

Bauhaus Buildings

 1 9 Gordon Street
MAP V1

This city block has asymmetrical balconies and a recessed left side. The concrete pergolas that criss-cross the roof are intended to act as sun-breakers.

Bauhaus building on Bialik Street

2 Bialik Street
MAP V3

This street is an architectural mix of 1930s Bauhaus and 1920s Eclectic style. No. 21 has clean lines accented by horizontal balcony roofs and vertical pillars. Inside, a Bauhaus Museum features 1930s furnishings. No. 18 has two balcony wings enclosing a central garden.

3 5 Frug Street
MAP V2

Known as the Thermometer House, this structure was designed for the local climate. Triangular slats supply light and shade to the stairwell.

4 Yael Street
MAP W2

No. 6 has asymmetrical windows and balconies within a symmetrical frame. No. 5 is all horizontal planes, except for the vertical stairwell with glass tiles and porthole windows that provide natural light and air.

5 12 Tel Hai Street
MAP W2

This building incorporates the boat shape conceptualized by Erich Mendelsohn, the first notable German-Jewish architect to arrive in Tel Aviv. The curves, designed to take the edge off the harshness of modern life, were criticized as being contrary to Bauhaus principles.

6 Dizengoff Square
MAP V2

Beautifully restored 1930s buildings grace this square, which is being restored. The Cinema Hotel, built as a movie theater in 1939, has ribbons of horizontal windows, overhanging ledges, and curved balconies.

7 65 Sheinkin Street
MAP V3

Built in 1935, the Rabinsky House uses practical fixtures to create decorative elements. The balconies are horizontal, with holes to allow the breeze to cool the building.

8 Ahad HaAm Street
MAP V4

No. 49 is a series of rounded corners set off by angular balconies. No. 57 is made up entirely of rectangles and cubes. No. 93, 95, and 126 have classic Bauhaus window strips.

9 Rothschild Boulevard

A perfect white cube sits at No. 71, with unbalanced windows and slit balconies. The Rubinsky House at No. 82 has a characteristic vertical glass stairwell. No. 142 has curved projecting balconies with balustrades, a flat roof, and cafés at ground level (see p83).

10 Mazeh Street
MAP W4

No. 41 was the first structure to be built on stilts in Tel Aviv. No. 56 sits in front of the Diaghilev Hotel, a late 20th-century block that echoes the structure of the original 1934 edifice.

Shopping Areas

1  **HaTachana**
MAP T5
Housed in the restored old Jaffa train station, this is a self-contained complex of designer boutiques, handmade jewelry stores, and a couple of great eating options.

2 **Shabazi Street**
MAP U4 ▪ Neve Tzedek
Fashion designers, jewelers, ceramicists, and shoe boutiques abound along this street. Great for a spot of window shopping.

3 **HaCarmel Market**
MAP V3 ▪ Open 8am–5pm Sun–Fri
The fresh produce section at this traditional souk is legendary. The side alleys specialize in spices, fish, nuts, and sausages.

4 **Gan HaHashmal**
MAP W4
Don't be discouraged by the seedy look; this is the place for cutting-edge fashion, jewelry, and footwear.

5 **Dizengoff Street**
MAP V2
This is Tel Aviv's main retail street. The Bauhaus Center at No. 99 is an essential stop for gifts, and Dizengoff Square has a flea market every Tuesday and Friday. Dizengoff Center mall is at the southern end.

6 **Nahalat Binyamin**
MAP V4 ▪ Open 9:30am–5:30pm Tue, 9am–4pm Fri
On Tuesday and Friday, this buzzing pedestrianized street hosts an arts and crafts fair. Glassware, jewelry, and Judaica are available.

Nahalat Binyamin objet d'art

7 **Azrieli Centre**
MAP X2 ▪ Adm to the observatory
These triangular, square, and circular space-age skyscrapers define the Tel Aviv-Jaffa skyline. There's a three-level shopping mall inside, and an observatory deck on the 49th floor of the round tower.

8 **Sheinkin Street**
MAP V3
Upscale Sheinkin used to be the hub of Tel Aviv's Bohemian fashion scene. Sidewalk cafés and independent boutiques and eateries still give the chain stores a run for their money.

9 **Artists' Quarter, Jaffa**
MAP S6
The lanes here are crammed with studios and galleries. Buy original works by the sculptor in the Ilana Goor Museum, or check out Israeli poster art at the Farkash Gallery.

10 **Flea Market, Jaffa**
MAP T6
Spread across the sidewalk or stacked onto stalls, genuine antiques can be found among the junk at this flea market, along with several vintage shops and quaint cafés.

Dizengoff Square flea market

See map on pp80–81

Bars and Nightlife Spots

José González of rock band Junip playing a gig at the Barby Club

1 Barby Club
MAP V6 ■ 52 Kibbutz Galuyot St ■ (03) 518 8123 ■ Open 8:30pm–late ■ barby.co.il

A magnet for Israeli musical talent, Barby is the best place in the city to hear both up-and-coming bands and established musicians.

2 The Container
MAP S6 ■ Warehouse 2, Jaffa Port ■ (03) 683 6321 ■ Open noon–late Sun–Thu, 10am–late Fri & Sat

This popular "project space," located in one of the converted warehouses on the port, blends live music shows and art with food and alcohol.

3 Shaffa Bar
MAP T6 ■ 3 Rabbi Nachman St, Jaffa ■ (03) 681 1205 ■ Open 9am–late daily

At Jaffa's flea market, this is a Mediterranean café by day and a trendy bar with live music at night.

4 Suramare
MAP X3 ■ 24 Seadia Gaon St ■ (054) 531 2553 ■ Open 8:30pm–late

Trendy rooftop bar with olive trees that enhance the unique atmosphere.

5 Mike's Place
MAP U2 ■ 90 Herbert Samuel St ■ (03) 510 6392 ■ Open 11am–late

With a great beach location and a young vibe, this bar attracts an international crowd with its cheap drinks, diner and Tex-Mex food, and live music (nightly at 10pm).

6 The Cat & The Dog
MAP X3 ■ 23 Carlebach St ■ (03) 561 5595 ■ Open 11pm–7am daily

Underground club playing electronic music, popular with those who like to drink and party through the night.

7 Lima Lima Bar
MAP V4 ■ 42 Lilienblum St ■ (054) 246 7906 ■ Open 10:30pm–5am daily

This dance bar and lounge is famous for its theme nights, including epic, gay-friendly hip-hop on Mondays.

8 HaMinzar
MAP V3 ■ 60 Allenby St ■ (03) 517 3015 ■ Closed Yom Kippur

This characterful bar is cheap and a bit grungy, but it's one of the best hangouts in the city to meet people. Excellent bar food.

9 Imperial Craft Cocktail Bar
MAP U2 ■ 66 HaYarkon St ■ (073) 264 9464 ■ Open 6pm–late daily

Voted one of the world's 50 best bars in 2015, this cozy spot is best known for fabulous cocktails – try the Spicy India or the World Peace Martini.

10 Radio EPGB
MAP W4 ■ 7 Shadal St ■ (03) 560 3636 ■ Open 9pm–7am daily

For a slightly alternative, underground, hip night out, this place is recommended for its music. Different DJs every night.

Places to Eat

1 Toto
MAP X2 ▪ 4 Berkovich St
▪ (03) 693 5151 ▪ Open noon–
midnight daily ▪ $$$

With gourmet Mediterranean dishes, Toto is great for business lunches as well as a romantic date night.

2 HaAchim
MAP W3 ▪ 12 Ibn Gabirol St
▪ (03) 691 7171 ▪ Open noon–midnight
Sun–Thu, from 9am Fri–Sat ▪ $$

Locals flock here for creative meat, seafood, and vegetarian dishes inspired by Greece and the Levant.

3 The Norman
MAP W4 ▪ The Norman Tel Aviv, 23–5 Nachmani St ▪ (03) 543 555 ▪ Open daily ▪ $$$

This gourmet place serves Franco-Mediterranean food with a Niçoise flavor – and a very Israeli twist.

Courtyard seating at The Norman

4 HaHalutzim 3
MAP V5 ▪ 3 HaHalutzim St
▪ (03) 523 1016 ▪ Closed Sat–Sun & lunch Mon–Thu ▪ $$

In the lively Shuk Levinsky section of South Tel Aviv, this relaxed little place is both a neighborhood bistro and a bar. The food is unpretentious, the soundtrack classic jazz.

5 HaBasta
MAP V3 ▪ 4 HaShomer St ▪ (03) 516 9234 ▪ Closed Sat eve ▪ $$$

In Tel Aviv's main food market, Shuk HaCarmel, this intimate, bistro-style

restaurant uses the freshest seasonal ingredients for French-inspired cuisine. It's also a wine bar.

6 Nanuchka
MAP V4 ▪ 30 Lilienblum St
▪ (03) 516 2254 ▪ Open 11–5am daily
▪ $$

A classy bar-restaurant specializing in Georgian cuisine, part of the city's flourishing vegan scene.

7 Raphaël
MAP U2 ▪ 87 HaYarkon St
▪ (03) 522 6464 ▪ Open noon–4pm & 7–11pm daily ▪ $$$

The traditions of France and North Africa inspire this upscale standard-bearer of New Israeli cuisine.

8 Taizu
MAP W4 ▪ 23 Menahem Begin St ▪ (03) 522 5005 ▪ Open noon–3:30pm Thu–Sat & 6:30pm–midnight daily ▪ $$

This innovative "AsiaTerranean" restaurant uses local ingredients for its dishes inspired by Southeast Asian, Indian, and Chinese food.

9 Kitchen Market Tel Aviv
MAP E3 ▪ Hangar 12, Tel Aviv Port ▪ (03) 544 6669 ▪ Closed lunch Sun ▪ $$

Overlooking the sea, this local foodies' haunt serves Mediterranean dishes, all made with fresh seasonal produce from the farmers' market downstairs.

10 Yaffo Tel-Aviv
MAP E3 ▪ 98 Yigal Alon St
▪ (03) 624 9249 ▪ Open daily ▪ $$$

This celebrated restaurant offers a mix of Italian form and Israeli creativity inspired by chef Haim Cohen's rich culinary biography.

See map on pp80–81

🔟 Galilee and the North

Capital, Capernaum synagogue

This is the greenest region of Israel, with lush valleys and wooded hills. Brimming with wild flowers in spring and crisscrossed by hiking trails, it is also a good place for horseback riding and bird-watching. The sparkling Sea of Galilee is a major draw, and Tiberias makes a good base for exploring sites central to Jesus' ministry. The region is steeped in Jewish religious history too. The town of Safed has winding streets and ancient synagogues, while the region's wealth of archeological sites – Caesarea, Beit She'an, and Tzipori – is overwhelming. A visit to Akko is like stepping back in time, and nearby Haifa is bright and bustling. The Golan Heights has spectacular views, while majestic Mount Hermon has a winter ski slope.

GALILEE AND THE NORTH

① **Top 10 Sights**
see pp91–3

① **Places to Eat**
see p95

① **Archeological Sites**
see p94

Previous pages The distinctive Monastery of the Twelve Apostles, near Capernaum

1 Haifa

The focal point of this port city, built on and around the slopes of verdant Mount Carmel, is the Baha'i Gardens, containing the golden Shrine of the Bab. In the German Colony, Ben-Gurion Street is lined with attractive Templer buildings, many of which have been turned into restaurants, bars, or hotels. Haifa has a mixed population, and the lanes of the Arab area of Wadi Nisnas contain great local eateries. The Carmel Center district, high atop Mount Carmel, has some excellent restaurants, while the port is popular for its nightlife. Museum buffs will be spoiled for choice, as the city boasts excellent art, science, and maritime museums *(see pp24–5)*.

2 Northern Golan

MAP A6 ■ Adm for Nimrod Castle, Banias Nature Reserve, and Mount Hermon ■ www.parks.org.il

Captured from Syria in 1967, the Golan is known for stunning scenery and dramatic viewpoints. The peak of Mount Hermon has skiing in winter *(see p50)*, while Nimrod Castle is a superbly located Crusader-era Muslim fortress. The waterfalls, walks, and archeological sites at Banias Nature Reserve are fun for all ages. Boutique industries flourish in *moshavim* and kibbutzim in the area, while four Druze villages and towns, including Majdal Shams and Mas'ade, welcome visitors to their grilled-meat restaurants and specialty baklava shops.

The Franciscan church in Cana

3 Cana (Kafr Kana)

MAP C5 ■ Churches St ■ **Franciscan Church of the Wedding Feast: open 8am–noon & 2–5pm Mon–Sat; Greek Orthodox Wedding Church: open 8am–3pm Mon–Sat, closed Sun afternoon**

Tradition holds that Jesus turned water into wine in this large Arab village, 6 miles (10 km) north of Nazareth's Old City. Two churches compete to commemorate the event. The Franciscan church has an ancient mosaic and crypt, but the more ornate Greek Orthodox church contains stone jars that are said to have been involved in the miracle itself.

Spectacular viewpoint, Northern Golan

4 Southern Golan
MAP B6 ■ www.parks.org.il

Some of Israel's best hiking is here, in the Yehudia Nature Reserve. The Zavitan Canyon leads to pools with extraordinary hexagonal basalt formations, while Yehudia Canyon entails swimming through pools of icy water. Katzrin, the regional capital, was founded in 1977. There's an ancient Jewish settlement, an archeological museum, and a visitor center here. Gamla Nature Reserve also has walking trails.

5 Sea of Galilee
A popular holiday spot, this scenic lake is called the Kinneret by Israelis *(see pp32–3)*. Major Christian sites dot the banks. At Tabgha, a church marks the traditional site of the Feeding of the Five Thousand. Capernaum has archeological remains, including a church built over the house of the Apostle Peter. The Mount of Beatitudes has an octagonal church and sublime views. At Yardenit, on the south side of the lake, white-gowned pilgrims gather to be baptized in the Jordan River.

6 Tiberias
MAP C5 ■ Tourist Office: 23 HaBanim St; (04) 672 5666

This large resort town was founded in Roman times to take advantage of the nearby hot springs. These remain an attraction, as do the nearby beaches. Roman ruins at Hamat Tiberias National Park include a zodiac wheel mosaic in the synagogue. One of four Jewish holy cities, Tiberias has tombs of many eminent rabbis.

Ancient mosque, Tiberias

The colorful harbor at Akko's Old City

Old mosques join the Protestant, Catholic, and Greek churches on the water's edge.

7 Jezreel Valley
MAP C5 ■ Kavim buses 411 and 412 to Beit She'an

The valley is edged to the south by the Gilboa mountains, with its scenic driving route, walking trails, and viewpoints. Ruins of the Roman city of Beit She'an *(see p94)* at the valley's eastern end are the most extensive in the country. The natural pools at Gan HaShlosha National Park are perfect for bathing, while close by, the Beit Alpha synagogue *(see p94)* has a magnificent Byzantine-era mosaic floor. There's an art museum and a lovely café at Kibbutz Ein Harod Meuchad.

8 Safed (Tzfat)
MAP B5 ■ Synagogues: Open 9:30am–5pm Sun–Thu (till noon Fri); Beit HaMeiri Museum: 8:30am–2:30pm Sun–Thu (till 1:30pm Fri)

Sephardic Jewish scholars fleeing the Spanish Inquisition turned Safed into a world center of Kabbalah (Jewish mysticism), and it retains an ethereal vibe to this day. Centuries-old synagogues associated with illustrious rabbis from centuries past are still in use, while the Artists' Quarter is crammed with galleries and studios. For a glimpse into 19th-century life here, drop by the Beit HaMeiri Museum.

9 Akko (Acre)

MAP B4 ■ Visitor Center,
Festival Garden ■ (1700) 708 020
■ Most sites open 8:30am–4/5pm daily

The mostly Arab Old City, enclosed
by solid walls, a broad moat, and the
Mediterranean, has a citadel, souk
(market), mosques, Turkish *khans*,
and a hammam from the 1700s;
hidden deep below is a subterranean
Crusader city. Old Akko has great
fish restaurants near the harbor and
a famous hummus joint. The lovely
Baha'i Gardens outside the city hold
the Baha'i faith's most sacred site.

CHRIST'S MINISTRY

Jesus did much of his preaching by the
shores of the Sea of Galilee. It is where
he is believed to have walked on water,
fed the 5,000, given the Sermon on the
Mount, and expelled a legion of devils.

10 Nazareth

MAP C5

Israel's largest Arab city is best
known as Jesus' childhood home.
Most of the major Christian sites and
the souk are in the bustling Old City,
a maze of alleyways between the
Greek Orthodox Church of the
Annunciation (Church of St. Gabriel)
and the Catholic Basilica of the
Annunciation *(see p42)*. Hidden down
narrow passages are the Synagogue
Church, the White Mosque, Ottoman-
era mansions, and great restaurants.

A WALKING TOUR OF SAFED

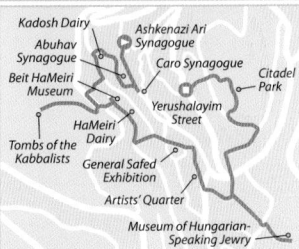

▶ MORNING

Start at the elaborately painted
Ashkenazi Ari Synagogue,
founded in the 1500s and rebuilt
after the great earthquake of
1837. Walk south through the
Synagogue Quarter, past beautiful
Judaica shops, to the **Caro
Synagogue**, named after
Rabbi Yosef Caro, compiler of
an important code of Jewish law.
Backtrack a bit and head down
the hill to the **Abuhav Synagogue**,
endowed with an ornately carved
modern courtyard. Stop off at
Kadosh Dairy for a cheesy snack
on the way to the **Tombs of the
Kabbalists**, among them the Ari.

AFTERNOON

 After a picnic lunch of *g'vina
Tzfatit* (a local cheese) from at
HaMeiri Dairy, visit the **Beit
HaMeiri Museum** for a look at
life in the city during Ottoman
times. Then walk to the **Artists'
Quarter**, home to the General
Safed Exhibition, which exhibits
a selection of works by some
60 local artists. Visit individual
artists' studios to see paintings,
calligraphy, ceramics, glasswork,
and sculpture, much of it with
a Jewish mystical theme.
Then, for something completely
different, head to the **Museum
of Hungarian-Speaking Jewry**,
whose evocative exhibits focus
on the richness of Jewish culture
in parts of Central Europe. Enjoy
a casual dinner of shawarma or
falafel on **Yerushalayim Street**
after walking through the **Citadel
Park**, a Crusader fortress at the
highest point in town.

See map on p90

Archeological Sites

1 Beit Alpha Synagogue
This 5th-century synagogue has an almost intact mosaic floor showing the Ark of the Covenant and a zodiac wheel design *(see p44)*.

2 Belvoir Castle
MAP C5 ▪ Off Route 90, 17 miles (27 km) S of Tiberias ▪ (04) 658 1766

This well-preserved Crusader fortress evokes the siege by Saladin's armies that ended in 1189 with the surrender of the Christian defenders.

3 Megiddo National Park
MAP C4 ▪ Route 66, 22 miles (35 km) SE of Haifa ▪ (04) 659 0316

According to the Book of Revelation, this is where Armageddon (Megiddo) will take place. Archeologists have found over 24 different historical layers, some as far back as 4000 BC.

4 Nimrod Castle
MAP A6 ▪ NE of Banias ▪ (04) 694 9277

Perched atop a narrow ridge, this 13th-century castle was built by Muslim rulers. The walls are well preserved, and the views astounding.

5 Beit She'an Ruins
MAP D5 ▪ (04) 658 7189

Israel's best-preserved Roman city boasts almost intact bathhouses, shops, and a theater.

6 Gamla Nature Reserve
MAP B6 ▪ Route 808, Lower Golan

In AD 67, thousands of Jewish rebels held out here for seven months under Roman siege. The park's cliffs host nesting vultures, and there are also waterfalls.

7 Tzipori National Park
The Roman and Byzantine town of Tzipori (Zippori) is famous for its extraordinary water-supply system and its mosaics *(see p44)*.

8 Banias Nature Reserve
MAP A6 ▪ Off Route 99, 9 miles (15 km) E of Kiryat Shmona ▪ (04) 690 2577

This popular park has walking trails that lead past Ptolemaic, Roman, Crusader, and Islamic remains.

9 Korazim National Park
Remains of dolmens, homes, ritual baths, and a synagogue can be seen in this ancient hillside Jewish town *(see p44)*.

10 Caesarea National Park
MAP D3 ▪ Off Rd 2 ▪ (04) 626 7080

Founded by Herod the Great and named for Augustus Caesar, this grand port city has extensive Roman ruins. Highlights include an amphitheater and the port itself.

Roman ruins at Caesarea

Places to Eat

PRICE CATEGORIES

For a three-course meal for one with half a bottle of wine (or equivalent meal), taxes, and extra charges.

$ under $25 $$ $25–55 $$$ over $55

① Helena, Caesarea National Park

MAP D3 ▪ Old Harbor ▪ (04) 610 1018 ▪ Open noon–11pm ▪ $$

Helena boasts an excellent location and top-notch Mediterranean food.

② Abu Ashraf, Nazareth

MAP C5 ▪ Diwan al-Saraya, Old City ▪ (04) 657 8697 ▪ Open 8am–8pm Mon–Sat, noon–4pm Sun ▪ $

Katayef, a Nazarene-style crêpe with either goat cheese or cinnamon walnuts inside, is the specialty here.

③ Al-Reda, Nazareth

MAP C5 ▪ 21 Al-Bishara St ▪ (04) 608 4404 ▪ Open 1pm–2am Mon–Sat, 7am–am Sun ▪ $$$

Traditional Nazarene dishes and Mediterranean cuisine are served beneath soaring ceilings in an 18th-century Arab mansion.

④ El Babor, Umm al-Fahm

MAP D4 ▪ Hwy 65 ▪ (04) 611 0691 ▪ Open 10am–11pm daily ▪ $$

This veteran Arab restaurant, founded in the 1980s, is famous for its grilled meats and superb selection of vegetarian *meze*.

⑤ The Witch's Cauldron and the Milkman, Nahal Nimrod

MAP A6 ▪ Upper Golan ▪ (04) 687 0049 ▪ Open noon–9pm Sun & Sat ▪ $$$

The focus here is on rich casseroles and dishes that use local ingredients.

⑥ HaAri 8, Safed

MAP B5 ▪ 8 HaAri St ▪ (04) 692 0033 ▪ Closed Fri, Sat ▪ $$

Grilled meats are the speciality at central Safed's most acclaimed restaurant, though vegetarians will have plenty to eat too, including generous salads, pasta, and soups.

⑦ Fattoush, Haifa

MAP C3 ▪ 38 Ben-Gurion St, German Colony ▪ (04) 852 4930 ▪ Open 9–1am ▪ $$$

Choose between outdoor seating or the candlelit cavern at Fattoush for Oriental and international cuisine.

Pleasant dining area at Fattoush

⑧ Uri Buri, Akko

MAP B4 ▪ HaHagana St ▪ (04) 955 2212 ▪ Open noon–11pm daily ▪ $$$

This fish and seafood restaurant in a seaside Ottoman mansion is magical. Try the chef's tasting menu.

⑨ Ma'ayan HaBira, Haifa

MAP C3 ▪ 4 Natanzon St ▪ (04) 862 3193 ▪ Open 10am–5pm Sun–Fri, 10am–11pm Tue, closed Sat ▪ $$

A Haifa institution for over half a century, this port-area pub is known for its beer and Jewish dishes from Eastern Europe.

⑩ Moshbutz, Moshav Ramot

MAP B6 ▪ Eastern Shore, Sea of Galilee ▪ (04) 679 5095 ▪ Open 6pm–late daily ▪ $$$

Succulent steaks from Golan-bred cattle attract carnivores from far and wide. The perfect complement for a meaty meal: a Golan wine.

See map on p90 ←

TOP 10 Dead Sea and the Negev

Rich in fascinating ancient sites, this region is where the Dead Sea Scrolls were discovered and Jewish rebels atop Masada defied the Romans. At the Dead Sea, spas and mineral-rich waters attract tourists and cure-seekers. Freshwater springs at Ein Gedi oasis create a surprising swathe of lush vegetation amid the arid hills. In the high Negev Desert, the vast crater of Makhtesh Ramon is best explored on foot. The Nabateans, builders of Petra, also established cities here, while at the southern tip of Israel, the resort city of Eilat is famed for its Red Sea coral reefs.

Entrance, Timna National Park

DEAD SEA AND THE NEGEV

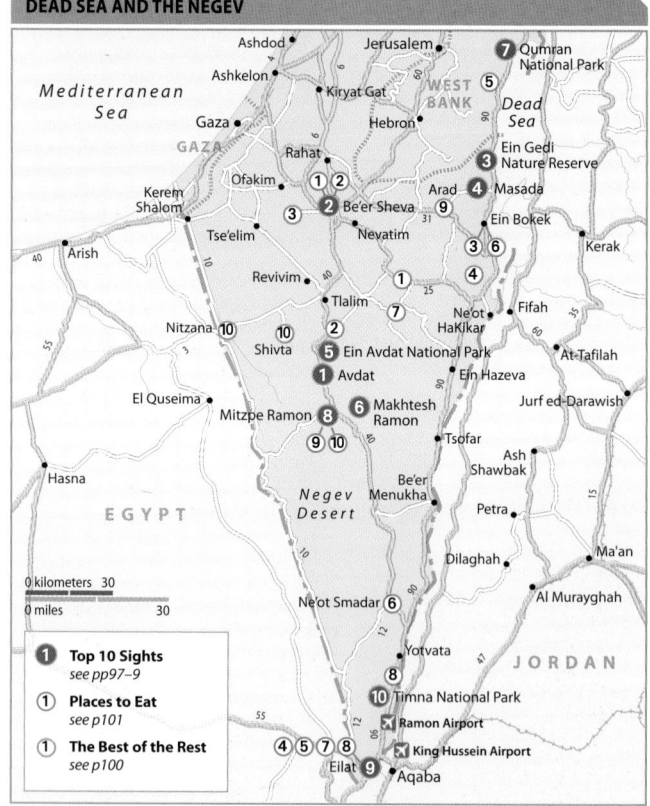

Top 10 Sights
see pp97–9

Places to Eat
see p101

The Best of the Rest
see p100

1 Avdat

MAP B2 ■ Route 40 ■ (08) 655 1511 ■ Egged bus 392, Metropoline bus 60 from Be'er Sheva ■ Open 8am–5pm (till 4pm Fri and winter) ■ Adm ■ www.parks.org.il

This settlement was founded in the 3rd century BC by the Nabataeans as a way station on the Spice Route. Now designated a UNESCO World Heritage Site, it sits on a hilltop overlooking desert canyons and an ancient network of irrigation canals. Many of the ruins here date from Byzantine times, including the remains of two churches and hundreds of cave dwellings.

2 Be'er Sheva

MAP H3 ■ Visitor Center: 1 Hebron Rd; (08) 623 4613; open 8am–5pm Sun–Thu, call in advance

Described in Genesis (21:22–34) as the place where Abraham dug a well, or be'er, the "capital of the Negev" is home to the main campus of the innovative Ben-Gurion University of the Negev. The former Governor's Residence, now the Negev Art Museum, and the mosque next door merit a special visit. Pick up a walking tour map at the Visitor Center. A Bedouin market is held in town every Thursday.

3 Ein Gedi Nature Reserve

MAP G5 ■ Route 90, 35 miles (56 km) S of Jericho ■ (08) 658 4285 ■ Open summer: 8am–5pm; winter: 8am–4pm ■ Adm ■ www.parks.org.il; www.ein-gedi.co.il

Fed by several springs, verdant Ein Gedi is like a slice of the tropics in

Botanical garden near Ein Gedi

the middle of the desert, at least as far as plant life is concerned. Two gorges, Wadi David and Wadi Arugot, can be walked along (and at some points splashed through), and animals, especially ibex and rock hyrax, can often be spotted. Kibbutz Ein Gedi, 2 miles (3 km) to the south, has a fabulous botanical garden and a lovely hotel (see p116), while Ein Gedi Health Spa is a fine spot to try mud treatments and soak in sulfur pools.

4 Masada

This World Heritage Site and national park towers over the western edge of the Dead Sea. At the end of the Jewish Revolt in AD 66–73, almost 1,000 rebels, besieged within this mountain fortress, killed themselves rather than submit to the rule of Rome. After the Romans left, the site was apparently deserted for 200 years, until, in the 5th century, Christian hermits established a monastery here. The remains of a Byzantine church can still be seen (see pp30–31).

Masada's mountaintop viewpoint

Hiking through the pale-walled ravines of Ein Avdat National Park

5 Ein Avdat National Park

MAP B2 ▪ Route 40, 32 miles (51 km) S of Be'er Sheva ▪ (08) 655 5684 ▪ Egged bus 392, Metropoline bus 60 ▪ Open summer: 8am–5pm; winter: 8am–4pm ▪ Adm ▪ www.parks.org.il

One of Israel's most stunning walks is along Ein Avdat's Nahal Zin gorge. The white-walled ravine has springs feeding ice-cold glassy pools. From the lower entrance, the walk passes a waterfall, a poplar grove, and rock-hewn steps before a final clamber up metal ladders to the upper car park. Ibex are often seen on the escarpment. The grave of David Ben-Gurion is located in Midreshet Sde Boker, next to the lower entrance.

6 Makhtesh Ramon

MAP B2 ▪ Route 40, 50 miles (80 km) S of Be'er Sheva ▪ Visitor Center: (08) 658 8691; open summer: 8am–5pm Sat–Thu; winter: 8am–4pm Sat–Thu; closes 1 hr earlier Fri ▪ Adm

Israel's version of the Grand Canyon, this is the largest erosion crater in the world, some 25 miles (40 km) long and 1,310 ft (400 m) deep. It is scattered with mountainous rock formations and laced with hiking and biking trails (take a map). Jeep tours, stargazing, and camping are also possible. In ancient times, the Nabataean Spice Route between Petra and Gaza crossed the crater.

7 Qumran National Park

MAP F5 ▪ Route 90, 12 miles (20 km) S of Jericho ▪ (02) 994 2235 ▪ Open summer: 8am–5pm Sat–Thu; winter: 8am–4pm Sat–Thu; closes 1 hr earlier Fri ▪ Adm

In 1947, a Bedouin shepherd found a cave full of jars containing the Dead Sea Scrolls. They had been hidden from the Romans 2,000 years ago by a desert community of ascetic Jews who awaited the Messiah. Many of the scrolls are on display in the Israel Museum *(see pp18–21)*, but here you can visit an archeological site and museum. Unless it's too hot, it is worth scrambling up to the caves themselves, but allow at least 2 hours and take lots of water.

THE DEAD SEA

No place on earth is lower than the Dead Sea, which is over 1,400 ft (427 m) below sea level. So while water flows into the Dead Sea, it cannot flow out. Over the eons, salts and minerals have accumulated, bringing the Dead Sea's salinity up to 34 percent, around ten times that of the ocean.

8 Mitzpe Ramon
MAP B2 ■ Route 40, 15 miles (24 km) S of Avdat ■ Egged bus 392, Metropoline bus 60 from Be'er Sheva

Perched at the rim of Makhtesh Ramon, this little town makes a great base for exploring the crater. Its industrial center has been revamped into the Spice Routes Quarter, with old hangars turned into boutique hotels, dance studios, restaurants, and shops.

9 Eilat
MAP D2 ■ www.coralworld.co.il

This Red Sea resort town draws visitors with its year-round sun, beaches, nightlife, and VAT-free shopping. The unbelievably diverse and colorful marine life makes for fabulous diving and snorkeling. At the Underwater Observatory Marine Park, you can see Red Sea corals and fish in their natural environment without getting wet. Trips to Petra can be easily organized in Eilat.

Colorful shoals of fish, Eilat

10 Timna National Park
MAP D2 ■ Route 90, 18 miles (29 km) N of Eilat ■ (08) 631 6756 ■ Adm ■ www.parktimna.co.il

This expanse of rocky desert holds archeological remains, stunning rock formations, and the oldest known copper mines in the world. Ancient Egyptians mined here around 1500 BC, and left two temples dedicated to the goddess Hathor. Solomon's Pillars offer stunning views, while the Mushroom Rock is a favored photo stop. A re-creation of the Tabernacle carried by the Israelites during the Exodus can be visited at set times.

ALONG THE DEAD SEA IN A DAY

▶ MORNING

Start with an early breakfast in Jerusalem, then drive 29 miles (47 km) east to the archeological site of **Qumran** (see p98); if the weather permits – it's often too hot – hike to the caves where the Dead Sea Scrolls were found. The next stop is the **Ein Gedi Nature Reserve** (see p97), where you can walk through one of the spring-fed wadis, spot desert wildlife, and visit ancient ruins, including a 5th-century synagogue. Spend at least a couple of hours here. In 2015 sinkholes forced the nearby Ein Gedi Beach and all its cafés to close, so for lunch – either sit-down or a picnic purchased at the grocery store – head to **Kibbutz Ein Gedi**, 2 miles (3 km) south. While there you can also visit the lovely **Botanical Gardens**.

AFTERNOON

After a short break from the midday sun, head 12 miles (20 km) farther south to the mountaintop fortress of **Masada** (see p97). Stop first at the excellent museum for some background, then take the cable car (or hike up the Snake Path) to the top to visit the evocative ruins, some built by Herod, others by the Jewish rebels. Take in the spectacular views across the Dead Sea to Jordan; see if you can spot, far below, the remains of eight Roman military camps. End the day at **Ein Bokek** (see p100), where, before dining at one of its several cafés or restaurants, you can enjoy floating in the briny waters of the Dead Sea – beach access is free to the public.

See map on p96 ←

The Best of the Rest

Nabataean ruins, Mamshit

1 Mamshit National Park
MAP A2 ■ Route 25, 5 miles (8 km) S of Dimona ■ www.parks.org.il

This is Israel's best-preserved Nabataean city. The Negev Camel Ranch nearby has hourly camel treks (no pre-booking needed).

2 Ben-Gurion's Grave
Midreshet Sde Boker

Israel's first prime minister, David Ben-Gurion (1886–1973), is buried overlooking the sublimely beautiful desert landscapes of his beloved Negev.

3 Israel Air Force Museum
MAP H3 ■ Hatzerim Air Base, 6 miles (10 km) W of Be'er Sheva ■ Open 8:30am–4pm Sun–Thu

Dozens of historic fighter aircraft, including a Spitfire from 1948, captured Iraqi and Syrian MiGs, and various attack helicopters, relate the story of Israel's air force.

4 Mount Sodom
MAP H5 ■ Route 90, 31 miles (50 km) S of Ein Gedi

The starkly beautiful landscape around the southern tip of the Dead Sea is dominated by this 700-ft (213-m) ridge made almost entirely of salt and riddled with caves. It can be explored on foot or by Jeep tour.

5 Metzukei Dragot Viewpoint
MAP G5 ■ 11 miles (17 km) S of Einot Tzukim

A steep road leads to the top of sheer cliffs, with breathtaking views, especially in the afternoon, of the Dead Sea and mountains in Jordan.

6 Ein Bokek
Set on the shore of the Dead Sea's southern basin, this strip is the main resort district. A dozen fancy hotels offer spa and mud treatments. There's a free public beach.

7 HaMakhtesh HaGadol and HaMakhtesh HaKatan
MAP A2 ■ Route 225, 4 miles (7 km) SE of Yerucham

These two erosion craters offer trekking, scattered ruins, and great views. Drive across the HaMakhtesh HaGadol and to a spellbinding view-point over the HaMakhtesh HaKatan.

8 Hai-Bar Yotvata Wildlife Reserve
MAP C2 ■ Route 90, 22 miles (35 km) N of Eilat ■ www.parks.org.il

Animals mentioned in the Bible and other endangered species are bred here, including Persian leopards, Arabian oryx, and Nubian ibex.

9 Arad
MAP H4

This town set on a desert plateau has a small artists' quarter and good hiking. Tel Arad, 5 miles (8 km) away, was a major city in the Canaanite and Israelite periods.

Oryx, Hai-Bar Yotvata Wildlife Reserve

10 Shivta National Park and Tel Nitzana
MAP B1 ■ www.parks.org.il

These remote Nabataean city ruins are rarely visited. Shivta (1st century BC) has three Byzantine churches.

Places to Eat

PRICE CATEGORIES

For a three-course meal for one with half
a bottle of wine (or equivalent meal),
taxes, and extra charges
....
$ under $25 $$ $25–55 $$$ over $55

1 Yakuta, Be'er Sheva
MAP H3 ▪ 27 Mordey Hagetaot
▪ (08) 623 2689 ▪ Open noon–
midnight Sun–Thu, noon–3pm Fri,
sundown–midnight Sat ▪ $$$

Authentic Moroccan-Jewish cuisine,
including couscous, grilled meats,
and slow-cooked Moroccan tagines,
are served in a sumptuously deco-
rated dining room.

2 Little India, Be'er Sheva
MAP H3 ▪ 15 Ringelblum St
▪ (08) 648 9801 ▪ Open noon–11pm
Sun–Thu, noon–3pm Fri ▪ $

This casual place has vegetarian and
some fish dishes. The Israeli-Indian
owner has added Jewish touches
alongside classic Indian cuisine.

3 Taj Mahal, Ein Bokek
MAP H5 ▪ Leonardo Inn ▪ (050)
999 0929 ▪ Open noon–midnight
daily ▪ $$

Arabic cuisine and a few Western
dishes (but nothing Indian)
are served in a poolside
Bedouin tent.

4 Lalo, Eilat
MAP D2 ▪ 259
HaHorev St ▪ (08) 633 0578
▪ Closed eves, Fri, Sat ▪ $

The home-cooked dishes
include tagines, stuffed
vegetables, and fish done
the spicy Moroccan way.
A great budget choice.

5 Pastory, Eilat
MAP D2 ▪ 7 Tarshish St
▪ (08) 634 5111 ▪ $$–$$$

Serves Eilat's tastiest Italian cuisine,
including meat, home-made pastas,
fish and seafood dishes, and their
very own ice cream.

6 Pundak Ne'ot Smadar
MAP C2 ▪ Shizafon Junction,
Kibbutz Ne'ot Smadar ▪ (08) 635
8180 ▪ Open 7am–7pm Sun–Thu,
7am–3pm Fri, noon–6pm Sat ▪ $

A vegetarian roadside inn with a
delightful setting. There's a country
kitchen inside, and the organic ingredients are grown on the kibbutz.

7 The Last Refuge, Eilat
MAP D2 ▪ Almog Beach ▪ (08)
637 3627 ▪ Open 12:30–11pm ▪ $$$

High-quality seafood fills the vast
menu and servings are generous.
The Red Sea is just outside.

8 Casa do Brasil, Eilat
MAP D2 ▪ 3 Hativat Golani
Ave ▪ (08) 632 3032 ▪ Open noon–
midnight daily ▪ $$$

This South American grill specializes
in skewers of meat and slow-cooked
ribs, lamb, and chicken.

9 HaHavit, Mitzpe Ramon
MAP B2 ▪ 10 Nahal Tzihor St
▪ (08) 658 8226 ▪ Closed Fri, Sat lunch
▪ $$$

Renowned for serving excellent
home-made meat and vegetarian
dishes. Wide selection of beers.

Spectacular views from Rosemary Restaurant

10 Rosemary Restaurant, Mitzpe Ramon
MAP B2 ▪ 1 Beresheet Rd ▪ (08) 659
8004 ▪ Closed lunch ▪ $$$

Great views and gourmet dishes
make for a memorable experience.
Located in the Beresheet Hotel.

See map on p96

☷⓿ Petra

This spectacular Nabataean city was hewn out of red-rock mountains and sandstone gorges. The carved tombs and temples of one of the world's most atmospheric ancient sites have sparked travelers' imaginations since the city's rediscovery in 1812. Built between the 3rd century BC and the 1st century AD, Petra became the capital of a vast trading empire. The Romans annexed it in AD 106; later, the Byzantines built churches here; even the Crusaders passed through. Known as the "rose-red city," it has monumental façades that reflect the swirls of color that pattern the surrounding hills and valleys. The hiking here is excellent, with peripheral peaks, altars, and tombs offering greater challenges.

Archeological Museum relief

High Place of Sacrifice

① High Place of Sacrifice
MAP C3

This is the best preserved of Petra's sacrificial places, and is where animals and birds were sacrificed. At the summit, two 20-ft (6-m) free-standing stone obelisks have been hewn out of the rock. Nearby is the High Place itself, demarcated by a large courtyard with a squat offering table. Steps lead to the main altar, with a rectangular indentation in the top. The adjacent round altar has a channel leading to a basin, possibly used for draining away sacrificial blood.

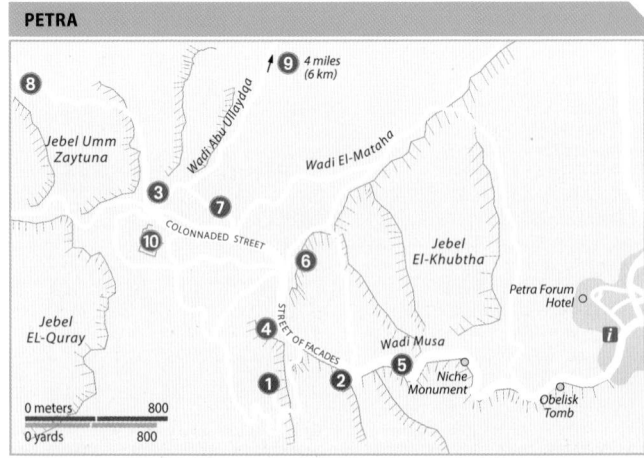

PETRA

Camels resting in front of the Treasury façade

(2) Treasury
MAP C3

Built in the 1st century BC, this is one of the most incredible sights in the Middle East. Its sudden materialization at the end of the Siq is unforgettable. The rose-pink façade, deeply recessed into the rock, is sharply chiseled into columns, two half-pediments, and horned capitals. The interior is simple by comparison. An outer court leads to the inner chamber with an ablution basin at the rear. Bedouins believed that the urn on top of the Treasury contained the hidden wealth of the pharaohs, so they shot at it in an attempt to dislodge it – hence the bulllet marks.

(3) Museums
MAP C3

The Archeological Museum is located inside a cave-tomb and displays relics excavated from the region. Stone statuary includes the elephant capitals used to decorate buildings. The newer Nabataean Museum puts the history of Petra into context. Among the artifacts displayed are jewelry, Edomite pottery, water pipes, figurines, and ancient coinage. Note the marble basin with lioness handles that was found inside Petra Church.

(4) Theater
MAP C3

Scooped out of the hillside, this Roman-style Nabataean theater has seating for 7,000 people. Above, you can see the inside of several tombs, cut into when the theater was built in the 1st century AD. Side tunnels allowed access to the stage, hidden from the Outer Siq by a wall.

(5) The Siq
MAP C3

The winding fissure of the Siq makes entering Petra truly romantic. In places it is so narrow it feels cave-like. Placing the Treasury at its exit was a calculated move for maximum visual impact. If you stay late at the site, walking back at sunset is a real highlight. The thrice-weekly night-time candlelit tours are magical.

The Siq, leading to the Treasury

REDISCOVERY OF PETRA

Hidden from the outside world for over 500 years, Petra was rediscovered by the Swiss explorer Johann Ludwig Burckhardt in 1812. On his travels, he was captivated by tales of a lost city in the mountains. Disguised as a Muslim scholar pretending to offer a sacrifice to the Prophet Aaron, he became the first modern Westerner to enter Petra.

6 Royal Tombs
MAP C3

The impressive scale of these tombs indicates that they were built for Petra's wealthiest citizens. The largest is the Palace Tomb. Originally five stories high, its top levels were raised up using huge blocks of stone. The Corinthian Tomb is badly eroded and asymmetrical, but its design echoes that of the Treasury. A staircase leads up to the lofty Urn Tomb, whose interior was consecrated as a church in AD 447. The beauty of these tombs is enhanced by the vibrant stripes of color rippling over their walls and ceilings. They are especially magnificent when viewed from a distance in the afternoon sun.

7 Petra Church
MAP C3

One of several churches, the main Byzantine basilica dates from the 5th and 6th centuries AD. The well-preserved mosaic aisle floors depict mythological creatures, deer, and birds, and are a highlight. Human figures represent the seasons and elements of nature. In the nave, parts of the geometrical stone and marble floor have also survived. In 1993, a cache of 152 burned scrolls was discovered here, giving insights into the daily life of Byzantine Petra.

Byzantine mosaic, Petra Church

8 Monastery
MAP C3

One of Petra's most mesmerizing sights, this temple is second only to the Treasury in impact. The path up to this site carved into the mountains ascends through a gorge and involves over 800 rock-cut steps. Dedicated to the deified king Obodas I, who died around 86 BC, it is of a similar design to the Treasury but simpler and on a larger scale. The façade hides one large chamber where an altar stood. The top is crowned by a colossal urn resting on ornate horned capitals.

The Monastery

9 Little Petra
5 miles (8 km) N of Wadi Musa

Siq al-Berid (Cold Canyon) is commonly known as "Little Petra," because it looks like a mini replica of the main city. A small gorge containing an unadorned temple leads to the town, which was possibly where Petra's wealthier merchants lived. Innumerable façades, temples, stairways, and cisterns reward exploration. A particular attraction is the Painted House, whose interior plasterwork is adorned with grapevines, flowers, and images of the Greek gods Eros and Pan.

The ruins of Little Petra

10 Qasr al-Bint
MAP C3

The fanciful Bedouin name "Qasr al-Bint al-Faroun" means the "Palace of the Pharaoh's Daughter." However, it is more likely that this grand edifice was Petra's most sacred temple, built in the 1st century BC. The impressive Temenos Gate signals your arrival at Qasr al-Bint's sacred precinct – it is still possible to make out remnants of the decorative plasterwork and marble veneers on the walls. The huge stone slab at the base of the steps was probably an altar to the sun god Dushara. The Crusaders used Qasr al-Bint as a stable.

WALK TO THE HIGH PLACE OF SACRIFICE

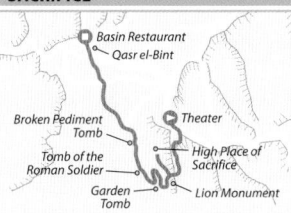

▶ MORNING

The High Place of Sacrifice was Petra's most important sacrificial center. Two paths lead to it today, and the round trip takes between 2 and 3 hours. The more impressive route begins shortly before the **Theater** *(see p103)*, marked at the start by **Djinn Blocks** *(see p35)*. The ascent is gradual but taxing. The summit, at 3,000 ft (914 m), is marked by a large terrace and two obelisks. Further north, a second plateau contains a rock-cut cistern and the two sacrificial altars of the High Place of Sacrifice. The views are exceptional, stretching all the way to Aaron's Tomb, a white shrine at the top of Petra's highest peak.

Follow the other path back down, which finishes in Wadi Farasa *(see p105)* near **Qasr al-Bint**. Steps go past the Lion Monument representing the goddess al-Uzza; water once poured from the lion's mouth. A series of steps then leads past colored rocks to the sheltered Garden Tomb, which is topped by a cistern. Further along, the Tomb of the Roman Soldier is named after the figure of a Roman official that is carved into a niche. A Triclinium, located on the opposite side of the tomb, has an ornately carved interior. Down the path is the Broken Pediment Tomb, followed by the Renaissance Tomb. Three urns adorn the arched entrance. The track widens here, leading visitors back to the city of **Petra**. Stop for a bite at the Basin Restaurant at the far end of the city before leaving.

See map on p102

Streetsmart

Bread on display at a baker's
in Jerusalem's Old City

Getting To and Around Israel and Petra

Arriving by Air

Located 32 miles (51 km) northwest of Jerusalem and 15 miles (24 km) southeast of Tel Aviv, **Ben Gurion International Airport** is served by many international airlines. **Air Canada**, **Delta**, **United**, and **El Al** (Israel's privatized flag carrier) offer non-stop flights from North America. European cities are linked by El Al and low-cost European carriers such as **Vueling**, **Air Berlin**, **easyJet**, **Wizz Air**, and **TUIfly**, as well as the Israeli carriers **Arkia** and **Israir**. From Asia, El Al and airlines such as **Korean Air** and **Cathay Pacific** offer direct flights to Tel Aviv. From Asia, often the cheapest route to Israel is on an Arab Gulf carrier and **Royal Jordanian** via Dubai, Abu Dhabi, or Doha to Amman.

To get from Ben Gurion to Jerusalem, taxis are available, but the cheapest way is to take a **Nesher** *sherut* (shared minibus). These run 24 hours, and go direct to your destination in the city. Book the day before when returning to the airport. Alternatively, take Afikim bus 485, which costs $4.50, or use the high-speed train line due to open in April 2018. Tel Aviv and Haifa are also linked to the airport by fast, comfortable trains that run 24 hours a day except on Shabbat (in practice, mid-afternoon Friday to sunset Saturday) and Jewish holidays.

Ben Gurion has the world's tightest airport security, so arrive three hours before departure.

Traveling to Petra

The easiest way to get to Petra from Israel is by organized tour, which removes the hassle of border crossings, visas, and transportation in Jordan. If you do decide to travel independently, on-arrival tourist visas can be issued at the Jordan River/Sheikh Hussein Crossing, about 19 miles (30 km) south of the Sea of Galilee. You need to pre-arrange a Jordanian visa to use the Allenby/King Hussein or Yitzhak Rabin/Wadi Araba crossings.

Getting Around by Train

Israel Railways serves over 60 destinations, from Nahariya and Beit She'an in the north, to Dimona and Be'er Sheva in the south. Almost all lines pass through Tel Aviv-Jaffa. The lovely coastal line is convenient for Akko and Haifa. Trains are busy on Sunday morning and Thursday night, and they don't run on Shabbat and Jewish holidays.

Getting Around by Intercity Bus

Every part of Israel is served by comfortable, air-conditioned buses run by about 20 companies (the largest is **Egged**).

Tickets are sold by the driver (except for Egged services to Eilat, for which advance reservations are recommended). Most lines do not run on Jewish holidays or Shabbat. The **Public Transportation Information Center** website has details in English.

Getting Around by Minibus

Known in Hebrew as a *sherut* and in Arabic as a *servees*, these minibuses do not have fixed stops; riders signal the driver when they want to get on or off. With fares about the same as those on buses, *sheruts* are particularly useful on Shabbat, when they run between major cities and within central Tel Aviv-Jaffa.

Getting Around by Taxi

Taxis are generally white with a yellow rooftop sign that is lit up when available. Higher "Fare 2" rates apply from 9pm to 5:30am and on Shabbat and Jewish holidays. Insist that the driver use the meter (for travel to/from Ben Gurion Airport, most people use government-set fares).

In several Israeli cities riders can order a taxi through **Gett** (formerly GetTaxi); **Uber** recently launched its service in Tel Aviv. In Jerusalem, Israeli cabbies may sometimes refuse to go to East Jerusalem; Arab drivers are generally willing to go anywhere in the city.

Getting Around by Car

Renting a car can be a convenient and economical way to see the country. Be aware that drivers can be unpredictable, and in some areas roads may not be up to Western standards. Global car rental companies have offices in cities and at Ben Gurion Airport, but local outlets, such as **Eldan**, often offer better prices. Published rates exclude insurance and collision waivers and toll charges.

Bus Tours

Taking a bus tour can be an efficient way to visit several sights in a short period of time. Tour companies include the popular **Abraham Tours**, **United Tours**, and **Egged**. For nature sites, the **Society for the Protection of Nature in Israel** has some excellent options.

Public Transport in Jerusalem

The city's ultramodern light rail (tram) line, run by **CityPass**, serves downtown West Jerusalem (Jaffa Road), the Old City's Damascus Gate, and Mount Herzl, as well as the Central Bus Station; buy tickets before boarding. Other parts of the city, including the Western Wall, are accessible by local Egged buses. A bus or tram trip costs about US\$1.50; drivers sell Egged's Rav-Kav Card. In East Jerusalem, buses to Arab towns in the West Bank leave from three stations located outside Damascus Gate; pay the driver when boarding.

Around Petra

Petra is best explored on foot. For the trip in, horse carriages can be hired at the Visitor Center (see p34), and it is also possible to get around by horse, donkey, or camel. Ensure that you negotiate your fee with the guide before you actually set out.

DIRECTORY

ARRIVING BY AIR

Air Berlin
w airberlin.com

Air Canada
w aircanada.com

Arkia
w arkia.com

Ben Gurion International Airport
c (03) 972 3333
w iaa.gov.il

Cathay Pacific
w cathaypacific.com

Delta
w delta.com

easyJet
w easyjet.com

El Al
w elal.com

Israir
w israirairlines.com

Korean Air
w koreanair.com

Nesher
w neshertours.co.il

Royal Jordanian
w rj.com

TUIfly
w tuifly.com

United
w united.com

Vueling
w vueling.com

Wizz Air
w wizzair.com

ARRIVING BY ROAD

Border Crossings
Allenby/King Hussein, Jordan River/Sheikh Hussein, Yitzhak Rabin/ Wadi Araba
w iaa.gov.il

GETTING AROUND BY TRAIN

Israel Railways
w rail.co.il/en

GETTING AROUND BY INTERCITY BUS

Egged
w egged.co.il

Public Transportation Information Center
w bus.co.il

GETTING AROUND BY TAXI

Gett
c 4717 2900
w gett.com/il

Uber
c 4717 2900
w uber.com

GETTING AROUND BY CAR

Eldan
w eldan.co.il

BUS TOURS

Abraham Tours
w abrahamtours.com

Egged Tours
w eggedtours.com

Society for the Protection of Nature in Israel
w natureisrael.org

United Tours
c 4717 2900
w unitedtours.co.il

PUBLIC TRANSPORT IN JERUSALEM

City Pass
w citypass.co.il

Practical Information

Passports and Visas

Visitors to Israel from almost all Western and Latin American countries receive a free 90-day tourist visa on arrival (sometimes travelers entering overland from Jordan are given 30 days). Travelers from most parts of Asia and Africa must request a visa from an Israeli consulate in their home country. For details, see the **Israeli Missions Around the World** website. In Israel, visa extensions are handled by the **Israeli Interior Ministry**. **Australia**, **Canada**, the **UK**, **US**, **New Zealand**, and other countries have embassies in Israel.

In Jordan, visitors from most countries are issued on-arrival tourist visas at Amman's Queen Alia Airport and the Jordan River/Sheikh Hussein border crossing. The fee of US \$56 is waived if you stay in Jordan for at least 2 consecutive nights. If using the Allenby/King Hussein or the Yitzhak Rabin/Wadi Araba crossing, you must arrange visas in advance. See the **Jordan Tourism Board** website.

To visit both Israel and Jordan, your passport must be valid for at least six months.

Travel Safety Advice

Get up-to-date travel safety information from the **US Department of State**, the **UK Foreign and Commonwealth Office**, and the **Australian Department of Foreign Affairs and Trade**.

Health

No vaccinations are necessary for visiting Israel or Petra (unless, for Jordan, you have been in a country with yellow fever in the past 10 days). If you require medical attention, Israel has some world-class hospitals, including Jerusalem's **Hadassah Medical Center** and the **Tel Aviv Sourasky Medical Center** (Ichilov Hospital) in Tel Aviv-Jaffa. Virtually all Israeli doctors speak English; clinics that cater specifically to English-speakers include the **Family Medical Center – Wolfson** in Jerusalem and **Tel Aviv Doctor** in Tel Aviv-Jaffa.

The most serious health threats faced by most visitors to Israel are heat stroke and dehydration. Drink lots of water all day and avoid the sun between 11am to 3pm, especially in desert areas. Tap water throughout Israel is drinkable; in Petra buy bottled water.

All cities and towns in Israel have pharmacies, some with extended hours. To find the nearest pharmacy that is open on Shabbat and Jewish holidays, ask at your hotel or consult the notice (in Hebrew) posted on the door of the nearest off-duty pharmacy.

Personal Security

Israel and Petra are generally very safe, even late at night. However, lone female travelers are occasionally subjected to verbal pestering and unwanted attention from local men. The problem is most acute in the Old City in Jerusalem. Don't walk alone in secluded areas after dark. In general, it's best to ignore catcalls.

Take the usual precautions against theft and be sure to obtain a police report you need to make an insurance claim.

Terrorist attacks almost never specifically target tourists, but it's a good idea to ask well-informed locals before venturing to sensitive places such as Jerusalem's Temple Mount and Hebron. Be prepared to have your bag searched at the entrances to bus and train stations, shopping malls, and supermarkets. Carry your passport at all times.

In the event of an emergency, call **Emergency Services, Israel** or the **Emergency Services, Jordan**.

Travelers with Special Needs

Museums, archeological sites, national parks, places to stay, and public spaces in Israel generally offer good accessibility to people with disabilities.

Appropriate Behavior

All holy sites and places of prayer – Jewish, Baha'i, Christian, and Muslim, – require visitors to dress modestly. Shorts and bare shoulders or upper arms are not acceptable, especially for women, and some Jewish sites will not admit women wearing trousers. Jewish sites may require head coverings for men (any hat is fine), while at Muslim holy places women may be asked to cover their heads with a scarf. You should also dress modestly when visiting Orthodox Jewish or traditional Muslim neighborhoods. Women might want to carry a wrap-around skirt and a headscarf with them.

Tel Aviv is among the world's top destinations for gay travelers, but in Jerusalem conservative attitudes make it unwise to flaunt same-sex – or, for that matter, heterosexual – relationships. In Palestinian areas and Jordan, homosexual relations are not socially acceptable,

and public displays of affection may cause offense and hostility.

Sources of Information

Websites with useful information include the **Israel Nature and Parks Authority** and the Israeli **Ministry of Tourism**, alongside **Travelujah** for Christian travelers. If visiting Tel Aviv-Jaffa, check out the **Tel Aviv Guide**, **Time Out Tel Aviv**, and **Visit Tel Aviv**. The **Visit Palestine** website is a great resource when visiting Palestinian Authority (West Bank) areas. Visitors to Petra should consult the Jordan Tourism Board and **Visit Petra** websites.

Currency and Banking

Israel uses the New Israel Shekel (NIS or ILS), which is divided into 100 *agorot*. Jordan has the Jordanian dinar (JD or JOR). Both currencies are used in the Palestinian Territories (West Bank). Credit cards, especially Mastercard and Visa, are accepted almost everywhere in Israel.

The easiest way to get cash is to use a debit card; most Israeli ATMs accept overseas cards. Cash can be exchanged without commission at a good rate at authorized exchange bureaux and some branches of the Israeli post office. Hotels generally offer poor rates of exchange.

DIRECTORY

PASSPORTS AND VISAS

Embassy of Australia
Tel Aviv-Jaffa
🔲 israel.embassy.gov.au

Embassy of Canada
Tel Aviv-Jaffa
🔲 israel.gc.ca

Embassy of the UK
Tel Aviv-Jaffa
🔲 ukinisrael.fco.gov.uk

Embassy of the US
Tel Aviv-Jaffa
🔲 il.usembassy.gov

Honorary Consulate of New Zealand
Tel Aviv-Jaffa
🔲 mfat.govt.nz

Israeli Interior Ministry
🔲 moin.gov.il (in Hebrew and Arabic)

Israeli Missions Around the World
🔲 embassies.gov.il

Jordan Tourism Board
🔲 visitjordan.com

TRAVEL SAFETY ADVICE

Australian Department of Foreign Affairs and Trade
🔲 dfat.gov.au
🔲 smarttraveller.gov.au

UK Foreign and Commonwealth Office
🔲 gov.uk/foreign-travel-advice

US Department of State
🔲 travel.state.gov

HEALTH

Family Medical Center – Wolfson
🔲 fmcwolfson.com

Hadassah Medical Center
🔲 hadassah-med.com

Tel Aviv Doctor
🔲 telavivdoctor.com

Tel Aviv Sourasky Medical Center
🔲 tasmc.org.il

PERSONAL SECURITY

Emergency Services, Israel
📞 Ambulance 102

📞 Fire 101
📞 Police 100

Emergency Services, Jordan
📞 Fire/Paramedics 199
📞 Police 191

SOURCES OF INFORMATION

Israel Nature and Parks Authority
🔲 parks.org.il

Ministry of Tourism
🔲 goisrael.com

Tel Aviv Guide
🔲 telavivguide.net

Time Out Tel Aviv
🔲 timeout.com/israel/tel-aviv

Travelujah
🔲 travelujah.com

Visit Palestine
🔲 visitpalestine.ps

Visit Petra
🔲 visitpetra.jo

Visit Tel Aviv
🔲 visit-tel-aviv.com

Internet and Telephone

High-speed Internet and Wi-Fi is available in virtually all cafés and places to stay. In some cities the municipal government provides free Wi-Fi in public spaces.

Israel's telephone country code is 972; the Palestinian Territories is 972 or 970 from some Arab countries; Jordan's country code is 962.

To call abroad, dial the access code of the company you prefer to use, such as **Cellcom**, **Golan Telecom**, and **Partner**.

Foreign cell phones generally work in Israel, but rates can be high, so it may make sense to buy a local prepaid SIM card from a service provider such as Cellcom, Golan Telecom, Partner, **HOT Mobile**, or **Pelephone**. You can also rent a local cell phone upon arrival at Ben Gurion Airport from companies such as **Global Cellular**.

TV, Radio, and Newspapers

The political and security situation in the region can change very rapidly, so it's a good idea to keep up with the news. In Israel, two English-language newspapers, *Haaretz* (left-of-center) and the *Jerusalem Post* (right-of-center), are published daily Sunday to Friday; both have websites that let you see the headlines for free. Online, you can also consult the *Times of Israel* and *Ynet News*.

The **Israel Broadcasting Authority** (IBA) has news broadcasts in English, available on TV channels 1 and 33, on the radio, and also online.

Opening Hours

In almost all Jewish areas, shops are closed on Shabbat, which lasts from sundown on Friday until an hour after sundown on Saturday. This means that shops, malls, and supermarkets are closed from 2 or 3pm Friday until Sunday morning. Shops may be closed on Sunday in Christian areas, and on Friday in Muslim areas.

Most eating places are open throughout the afternoon until late at night, including Shabbat. Except in hotels, almost all kosher restaurants are closed on Shabbat and Jewish holidays.

Israeli banks tend to work between 9am and 1pm Monday to Thursday.

Time Difference

Israel, the Palestinian Authority, and Jordan are three hours ahead of GMT, seven hours ahead of the US Eastern Standard Time, and 10 hours ahead of US Pacific Standard Time. Note that daylight savings begins and ends on different dates.

Weather

Most of Israel has a temperate, Mediterranean climate. July and August are very hot and humid on the Mediterranean coast and around the Sea of Galilee, and even hotter around the Dead Sea and in the Negev. Israel and Jordan get virtually no rainfall from May to September, while from December to February or March it can be chilly (and, on rare occasions, snowy) in Jerusalem but pleasant along the coast.

Even in winter, most days are fine in Eilat and Petra, which enjoy about 360 sunny days a year.

Shopping

Jerusalem's **Hutzot HaYotzer** (Artists' Colony), Nahalat Shiv'a neighborhood, and **Safed's Art Galleries** are among the best places in the world to purchase Judaica (Jewish ritual objects). Creative jewelry is available in boutiques around the country as well as at the **Nahalat Binyamin Arts and Crafts Fair** in Tel Aviv. Several enterprises in and around Jerusalem's Old City, including **Sandrouni** and **Balian Armenian Ceramics** sell authentic, hand-painted Armenian ceramics. The best place to look for designer clothing is Tel Aviv, especially along the northern section of Dizengoff Street. In Bethlehem and other parts of the West Bank, local products include figures made of carved olive wood, hand-blown Hebron glass, and Palestinian embroidery; there's a good selection at Bethlehem's **Palestinian Heritage Center**.

In souks (markets) such as in Jerusalem's Old City, haggling is de rigueur. Never accept the first price – it will be way over the odds. Compare prices, decide what you're prepared to pay, then make an offer well below that sum. Bargain firmly until both you and the vendor have arrived at a mutually agreeable price.

According to the **Israel Tax Authority**'s rules, tourists are entitled to a VAT (sales tax) refund when purchasing at least NIS400 of goods in an authorized store. Look for a sticker in the window and request a VAT refund invoice at the store for presentation at the airport or border counter alongside the goods.

Dining

Israel has a growing gourmet dining scene, with fusion food (sometimes called New Israeli cuisine) proliferating in Tel Aviv, Jerusalem, Haifa, and Nazareth. All around Israel, Mediterranean-style dishes are popular. Tel Aviv and Akko have excellent fish and seafood places. Several smaller restaurants specialize in traditional ethnic cuisines, including Moroccan, Persian, Ashkenazi, Kurdish, Yemenite, and Tripolitanian (Libyan). Levantine food dominates in Arab areas. Israel has some of the tastiest – and healthiest – street food, including some of the world's best hummus. The country also has one of the world's fastest-growing vegan cuisine cultures.

Some restaurants are kosher, including most places in West Jerusalem. This means that they follow Jewish dietary laws, serving either meat or milk products but not both, and they do not serve pork or seafood. Almost all kosher restaurants are closed on Shabbat, as well as on Jewish holidays.

In Israel, it is customary to leave a 10–15 percent tip for good service.

Accommodations

Accommodations in Israel range from international and stylish boutique hotels to hostels (check out **Israel Hostels** or the **Israel Youth Hostel Federation**) and other budget places. The **Society for the Protection of Nature in Israel** runs field schools with basic rooms, while some rural kibbutz guesthouses are quite luxurious (see **Kibbutz Hotels Chain**). B&Bs (*tzimerim* in Israel) mainly operate in the Galilee and Negev. The **Zimmeril** website is a handy resource for B&Bs and rural tourism.

Prices in Jerusalem, Bethlehem, and Petra are highest in June–August and around Jewish and Christian holidays. Booking ahead is always advisable, but essential during religious festivals.

DIRECTORY

INTERNET AND TELEPHONE

Cellcom
Int'l access code: 013
cellcom.co.il

Global Cellular
gcellular.net

Golan Telecom
Int'l access code: 016
golantelecom.co.il

HOT Mobile
Int'l access code: 017
hotmobile.co.il

Partner
Int'l access code: 012
partner.co.il

Pelephone
Int'l access code: 014
pelephone.co.il

TV, RADIO, AND NEWSPAPERS

Haaretz
haaretz.com

Israel Broadcasting Authority
iba.org.il/world

Jerusalem Post
jpost.com

Times of Israel
timesofisrael.com

Ynet News
ynetnews.com

SHOPPING

Balian Armenian Ceramics
armenianceramics.com

Hutzot HaYotzer
artistscolony.co.il

Israel Tax Authority
taxes.gov.il

Nahalat Binyamin Arts and Crafts Fair
nachlat-binyamin.com

Palestinian Heritage Center
palestinianheritage center.com

Safed's Art Galleries
safed.co.il

Sandrouni
sandrouni.com

ACCOMMODATIONS

Israel Hostels
hostels-israel.com

Israel Youth Hostel Federation
iyha.org.il.

Kibbutz Hotels Chain
kibbutz.co.il

Society for the Protection of Nature in Israel
natureisrael.org

Zimmeril
zimmeril.com

Places to Stay

PRICE CATEGORIES

For a standard double room per night (with breakfast if included), taxes, and extra charges.

....

$ under $110   **$$** $110–210   **$$$** over $210

Hotels in Jerusalem

Alegra Boutique Hotel

MAP F4 ▪ 13 Ha'achayot St, Ein Karem, West Jerusalem ▪ (02) 650 0506 ▪ www.hotelalegra. co.il ▪ $$$

Located 6 miles (10 km) west of the Old City, the Alegra is a boutique hotel with seven unique, luxurious rooms. There's also a spa and sauna, a sun roof, a lovely garden, and a top-class restaurant.

American Colony Hotel

MAP N1 ▪ 1 Louis Vincent St, Sheikh Jarrah, East Jerusalem ▪ (02) 627 9777 ▪ www.american colony.com ▪ $$$

This landmark hotel, founded in the late 1800s by devout Christians from Chicago, combines luxury, elegance, and true class, and has long been a favorite of journalists. The courtyard, garden, and Cellar Bar are a delight, and there's also a fitness center and a swimming pool (in season).

Dan Boutique

MAP N6 ▪ 31 Hebron Rd, West Jerusalem ▪ (03) 520 2552, (02) 568 9999 ▪ www.danhotels.com ▪ $$$

This hotel, located near the lively German Colony, is comfortable, jazzy, and informal. Standard rooms (and bathrooms) are a decent size and feature art and high-tech design.

Harmony Hotel

MAP M3 ▪ 6 Yoel Moshe Salomon St, Nachalat Shiva, West Jerusalem ▪ (02) 621 9999, (03) 542 5555 ▪ www.atlas.co.il ▪ $$$

The smooth white foyer sets the tone of this 50-room boutique hotel in the heart of the New City. The lounge has a pool table and outdoor seating. The breakfasts are great, as is the service. Free parking is available.

King David Hotel

MAP M5 ▪ 3 King David St, West Jerusalem ▪ (03) 520 2552, (02) 620 8888 ▪ www.danhotels.com ▪ $$$

This stately 1930s hotel, long the preferred lodging of presidents, prime ministers, and royalty, has splendid Old City views, an atmospheric terrace, a pool, and a grassy garden around the back. The plush rooms have antique furnishings; the service is impeccable.

Legacy

MAP N2 ▪ 29 Nablus Rd, East Jerusalem ▪ (02) 627 0800 ▪ www.jerusalem legacy.com ▪ $$$

This former YMCA in East Jerusalem, not far from the Damascus Gate, is a great mid-range option. Its institutional 1960s exterior hides an interior that is contemporary and bright, although some rooms are on the small side. The hotel also has an indoor pool.

Mamilla Hotel

MAP M5 ▪ 11 King Solomon St, West Jerusalem ▪ (02) 548 2200, (02) 548 2222 ▪ www.mamillahotel.com ▪ $$$

Chic and contemporary, with plenty of high-tech amenities, the Mamilla enjoys an excellent location near Jaffa Gate. Its drinking and dining options are superb – try the rooftop restaurant for views of the Old City.

Montefiore Hotel

MAP L4 ▪ 7 Shatz St, West Jerusalem ▪ (02) 622 1111 ▪ en.smarthotels. co.il ▪ $$$

Modern and gracious, this is great value, with comfortable beds and good bathrooms. Shatz Street has plenty of restaurants and shops to explore, and the Old City is nearby.

Mount Zion Hotel

MAP N6 ▪ 17 Hebron Rd, West Jerusalem ▪ (02) 568 9555 ▪ www.mount-zion.co.il ▪ $$$

Poised over Mount Zion and the Hinnom Valley, this hotel is within easy reach of both the Old City and downtown. The standard rooms are in the new wing, most of them facing the courtyard, while the citadel rooms are set in the historical wing. Suites and a villa are also available. There's a pool and a garden as well.

YMCA Three Arches
MAP M5 ▪ 26 King David St, West Jerusalem ▪ (02) 569 2692 ▪ www.ymca3arches.com ▪ $$$
Dedicated in 1933, this iconic building – known affectionately in Hebrew as Yimca – is visible all over town thanks to its 152-ft (46-m) tower. It's a great place to stay, with magnificent architecture, Mandate-era charm, and a reasonably priced restaurant too.

Hotels in Tel Aviv

Brown TLV Urban Hotel
MAP V4 ▪ 25 Kalisher St ▪ (03) 717 0200 ▪ www.browntlv.com ▪ $$$
A chocolate-brown color scheme sets the mood at this design hotel, as does the lovely staff. Artwork enhances public and private spaces, and there is a spa, a courtyard, and a sundeck. Standard rooms are a bit small, but the location near HaCarmel Market is spot on.

Center Chic Hotel
MAP V2 ▪ 2 Zamenhoff St ▪ (03) 526 6100 ▪ www.atlas.co.il ▪ $$$
Set in a striking Bauhaus building near Dizengoff Square, this is the sort of place where modern art adorns white brick walls. The flower-filled roof terrace has loungers and citrus trees. Breakfast is served at the adjacent Cinema Hotel.

The Diaghilev Live Art Boutique Hotel
MAP W4 ▪ 56 Mazeh St ▪ (03) 545 3131 ▪ www.diaghilev.co.il ▪ $$$
Set in a quiet leafy street, this contemporary hotel hosts art exhibitions. Accommodations are apartment-style, with kitchenettes and huge windows; rooms with balconies cost more. The airy foyer and rear deck are great spots to relax. Service is impeccable.

Gordon Boutique Hotel
MAP V1 ▪ 2 Gordon St/ 136 HaYarkon St ▪ (03) 520 6100 ▪ www.gordontlv.com ▪ $$$
Set by the beach, this ultramodern boutique hotel has 12 crisp rooms that are hip and high-tech. Some have sea views, though not all can be called spacious.

Market House Hotel
MAP T6 ▪ 5 Beit Eshel St ▪ (03) 797 4000 ▪ www.atlas.co.il ▪ $$$
Set in Jaffa Flea Market, this lavish hotel is built over a Byzantine church and has a glass floor to view the remains. It is a relaxing haven amid the bustling streets, and only a few minutes' walk from the Ottoman clock tower and the seafront.

Lodgings in Galilee and the North

Pilgerhaus Tabgha
MAP B5 ▪ Migdal-Tabgha, Galilee ▪ (04) 670 0100 ▪ www.heilig-land-verein.de ▪ $$
Located on the shores of the Sea of Galilee, this meticulously kept hotel is housed in a beautifully renovated building that dates from the 1880s. Its rooms are well appointed and modern, while the various outdoor areas – including the bar – are great for relaxation.

YMCA Peniel-by-Galilee
MAP C5 ▪ 3 miles (5 km) north of Tiberias ▪ (04) 672 0685 ▪ www.ymca-galilee.co.il ▪ $$
The foyer at this hotel is straight out of the British Mandate, while rooms are large but basic. The unruly gardens are lapped by the waters of the Sea of Galilee. Service isn't very polished but this is a quirky and restful place.

Akkotel
MAP B4 ▪ Salahuddin St, Old City, Akko ▪ (04) 987 7100 ▪ www.akkotel.com ▪ $$$
Set inside the walls that surround the Old City, this 16-room hotel has attentive staff, a family feel, and a splendid terrace. The quirky, pleasant rooms have all mod cons.

Colony Hotel
MAP C3 ▪ 28 Ben-Gurion Blvd, Haifa ▪ (04) 851 3344 ▪ www.colonyhaifa.com ▪ $$$
Set in the delightfully preserved, lively German Colony, this hotel has luxurious rooms with marble bathrooms, classy facilities and – if you're lucky – a balcony. The Baha'i Gardens dominate the view from the roof.

Mizpe Hayamim Spa Hotel
MAP B5 ▪ Midway between Safed and Rosh Pina, Upper Galilee ▪ (04) 699 4555 ▪ www.mizpe-hayamim.com ▪ $$$
Famed for its organic farm – orchards, dairy, vegetable gardens – which supplies its restaurant, this hotel has rooms with lovely views over the Galilee and a great spa.

Scots Hotel
MAP C5 ▪ 1 Gedud Barak Rd, Tiberias ▪ (04) 671 0701 ▪ www.scotshotels.co.il ▪ $$$

This deluxe hotel blends historic buildings with modern 5-star facilities. The "antique rooms" (1890s) with basalt stone walls are the most attractive, and the seasonal pool and terraced gardens are divine. Cultural events and brunches add to the atmosphere.

Villa Carmel
MAP C4 ▪ 1 Heinrich Heine St, off 30 Moriah Boulevard, Haifa ▪ (04) 837 5777/8 ▪ www.villacarmel.co.il ▪ $$$

Set in a 1940s building, this hotel is tucked away on the summit of Mount Carmel. The pleasant decor is enhanced by luxuriant bedding. The sundeck has a sauna and Jacuzzi, and the fragrant gardens are sublime.

Lodgings in the Dead Sea and the Negev

IYHA Masada Guesthouse
MAP H5 ▪ Masada ▪ (02) 594 5622 ▪ www.iyha.org.il ▪ $$ (dorms $)

This popular place, with a prime location at the foot of Masada, has well-equipped private rooms with air conditioning and TV as well as dorm beds. Book in advance.

Ein Gedi Country Hotel
MAP G5 ▪ Kibbutz Ein Gedi, Dead Sea ▪ (08) 659 4222 ▪ www.ein-gedi.co.il ▪ $$$

Set within lush gardens, this hotel boasts great views of the Dead Sea's desert landscape. The rooms all have quirky themes, and there's a seasonal pool. Use of the spa and admission to the nearby botanical garden are included in the room rate for hotel guests.

Herod's Palace
MAP D2 ▪ North Beach, Eilat ▪ (08) 638 0000 ▪ www.herodshotels.com ▪ $$$

Guests are pampered at this flashy, Las Vegas-style complex. While the rooms aren't as opulent as the public spaces, the adjacent beach, the huge swimming pool, and the in-house restaurants and bars are excellent.

Accommodations in Petra

Petra Palace Hotel
MAP C3 ▪ Wadi Musa ▪ (962) 3215 6723 ▪ www.petrapalace.com ▪ $

Located right in the center of Wadi Musa, with plenty of places to eat nearby, this modern, 200-room hotel has pleasant rooms and handsome, stone-paved public spaces. Amenities include an outdoor pool, and a Turkish-style spa with steam room, hot tub, and massages.

Rocky Mountain Hotel
MAP B3 ▪ Main St, Wadi Musa ▪ (962) 3215 5100 ▪ www.therockymountainhotel.com ▪ $

Modest but sociable place to stay, with an extremely helpful staff. Expect a good breakfast and amazing views from the terraces. It's a climb up from Petra but free shuttles are available.

Petra Guest House Hotel
MAP C3 ▪ Petra Entrance, Wadi Musa ▪ (962) 3215 6266 ▪ www.guesthouse-petra.com ▪ $$

An unbeatable location with friendly staff, modern facilities, and comfortable rooms, some of them remarkably spacious. The Cave Bar is in a Nabatean tomb-cave from the 1st century AD.

Mövenpick Resort Petra
MAP C3 ▪ Tourism St, Wadi Musa ▪ +962 3215 7111 ▪ www.movenpick.com ▪ $$$

The location of this resort, right next to the Siq, is unbeatable. There is a pool and several restaurants, including a fabulous roof terrace that's perfect for a drink after an exhausting day out.

Pilgrim Hospices in Jerusalem

Ecce Homo Convent Pilgrim House
MAP P4 ▪ 41 Via Dolorosa, Old City ▪ (02) 627 7292 ▪ www.eccehomopilgrimhouse.com ▪ $

Crucifixes adorn the walls, the terraces offer majestic views, and the staff are welcoming at this dignified pilgrim house. Rooms and dorms are spartan but good value. The complex incorporates the Ecce Homo Arch and a basilica.

Lutheran Guesthouse
MAP P4 ▪ 7 St. Marks St, Old City ▪ (02) 626 6888 ▪ www.guesthouse-jerusalem.com ▪ $

Set in the Old City's heart, this 1860 guesthouse

offers historic charm at reasonable prices. The spotless, air-conditioned rooms are grouped around a peaceful courtyard and there's a TV in the lounge.

Austrian Hospice

MAP P4 ■ 37 Via Dolorosa, Old City ■ (02) 626 5800 ■ www. austrianhospice.com ■ $$ (dorms $)
Built in 1857 in the style of a Viennese Ring palace, this "intercultural center" and hostel is great for independent travelers. It offers simple, comfortable rooms and dorms in a prime location. Gardens, a café-bar, and great views from the roof are added attractions.

Christ Church Guest House

MAP N4 ■ Omar Ibn al-Khattab Sq, Jaffa Gate, Old City ■ (02) 627 7727 ■ www.cmj-israel.org ■ $$
The location – just inside Jaffa Gate – couldn't be any better, and the guesthouse grounds are a peaceful haven. Rooms are simple but quaint. Unmarried couples are not allowed. There's an 11pm curfew.

St. Andrew's Scottish Guesthouse

MAP N6 ■ 1 David Remez St, West Jerusalem ■ (02) 673 2401 ■ www.scots-guesthouse.com ■ $$
Owned and run by the Church of Scotland, this small, peaceful guesthouse adjoins an austere Scottish church built in the late 1920s. Rooms have either garden or Old City views, while the terrace and colonial lounge are lovely spots for relaxing.

St. George's Cathedral Pilgrim Guesthouse

MAP N2 ■ 20 Nablus Rd, East Jerusalem ■ (02) 628 3302 ■ www.j-diocese. org ■ $$
Located near Damascus Gate, this Anglican-run guesthouse has a cloistered charm. The rooms are spacious, and some have Jerusalem-stone walls. Amenities include a courtyard garden and an atmospheric cathedral.

Notre Dame of Jerusalem Guesthouse

MAP N4 ■ 3 HaTzanchanim, West Jerusalem ■ (02) 627 9111 ■ www.notredame center.org ■ $$$
This magnificent, Vatican-owned edifice is just a few steps from New Gate, so the Old City views from the terrace of its wine-and-cheese restaurant are unsurprisingly great. The rooms are simple, the beds comfortable, and the breakfasts hearty.

Budget Stays

Abraham Hostel Jerusalem

MAP L2 ■ 67 HaNevi'im St, Davidka Sq, West Jerusalem ■ (02) 650 2200 ■ www.abraham hostels.com ■ $
An award-winning hostel catering brilliantly to independent travelers, with areas for socializing, a bar, free breakfast, laundry facilities, and excellent tours around the rest of the country. Accommodations include functional private rooms and dorm rooms of varying sizes.

Abraham Hostel Tel Aviv

MAP W4 ■ 21 Levontin St, Tel Aviv ■ (03) 624 9200 ■ www.abrahamhostels. com ■ $
Set just two blocks from Rothschild Boulevard and a 20-minute walk from the beach, the newest Abraham Hostel is an excellent place to relax and meet other travelers. There's a lounge, a bar, a kitchen for guests, laundry facilities, and a rooftop terrace; breakfast is included.

Citadel Youth Hostel

MAP J2 ■ 20 St. Mark St, Old City, Jerusalem ■ (02) 628 4494 ■ www.citadel youthhostel.com ■ $
Despite modest rooms and dorms, this warren-like hostel of Jerusalem stone has true character. Camp on the roof terrace in summer months.

Hayarkon 48

MAP U3 ■ 48 HaYarkon St, Tel Aviv ■ (03) 516 8989 ■ www.hayarkon48. com ■ $ (dorms $)
A hugely popular, veteran hostel near the beach, Hayarkon 48 has a sociable lounge and a well-equipped kitchen. It's a great spot for independent travelers.

Fauzi Azar Inn

MAP C5 ■ Nazareth ■ (04) 602 0469 ■ www. fauziazarinn.com ■ $$ (dorms $)
Located in a gorgeous 18th-century Arab mansion hidden away in an Old City alley, this inn is under Arab-Jewish management. With characterful private rooms and good-value dorms, it makes a superb base in Nazareth.

For a key to hotel price categories see p114

Index

Acknowledgments

Author

A British travel writer, researcher, and editor, Vanessa Betts has spent over 15 years working overseas. She has lived in Egypt, India, Israel and Singapore, and authored several guidebooks covering these areas. She currently splits her time between Asia, Egypt, and the UK.

Additional contributor

David Robinson's award-winning travel writing has appeared in dozens of guidebooks and has been featured in The New York Times, The Los Angeles Times, and National Geographic Traveler. During two decades in Tel Aviv, he worked on a PhD in late Ottoman history, covered security issues as an Associated Press Stringer, and helped lead the city's Critical Mass campaign for bike paths.

Publishing Director Georgina Dee

Publisher Vivien Antwi

Design Director Phil Ormerod

Editorial Sophie Adam, Ankita Awasthi Tröger, Kate Berens, Michelle Crane, Rachel Fox, Priyanka Kumar, Sally Schafer, Rachel Thompson

Cover Design Richard Czapnik

Design Hansa Babra, Tessa Bindloss, Marisa Renzullo, Ankita Sharma, Priyanka Thakur

Commissioned Photography Idris Ahmed, Steve Gorton

Picture Research Taiyaba Khatoon, Ellen Root, Rituraj Singh

Cartography Subhashree Bharti, Suresh Kumar, Stuart James, Casper Morris Base mapping supplied by Huber Kartographie.

DTP Jason Little

Production Stephanie McConnell

Factchecker Simon Griver

Proofreader Clare Peel

Indexer Helen Peters

Picture Credits

The publisher would like to thank the following for their kind permission to reproduce their photographs:
Key: a-above; b-below/bottom; c-centre; f-far; l-left; r-right; t-top

123RF.com: Ievgenii Fesenko 10c.

Alamy Stock Photo: age fotostock 80tl; Nir Alon 18bc; Stefano Baldini 74tl; Eddie Gerald 55cl, 85bl; Granger Historical Picture Archive 44cb; Yagil Henkin - Images of Israel 16br; Heritage Image Partnership Ltd 38br; Hanan Isachar 24c, 32cla, 60tr; Michael Jacobs 57cl, 83cla; Fabian Koldorff 75tr; LOOK Die Bildagentur der Fotografen GmbH 101crb; mauritius images GmbH 32crb; Middle East 11cr; Sean Pavone 4t, 22-3; PhotoAlto sas 57tr; PhotoStock-Israel 7tr, 82tl; PS-I 91b; Robert Preston Photography 4b; Robertharding 3tr, 106-7; Eitan Simanor 54t; Jack Sullivan 47br; WENN UK 52bc; www.BibleLandPictures.com 11bl; Y.Levy 59cl; Didier Zylberyng 105cl.

AWL Images: Jon Arnold 4crb; Michele Falzone 103t; Neil Farrin 12br; Gavin Hellier 2tr, 4cla, 36-7; Hemis 4cr, 7b, 10crb; Nigel Pavitt 104b, Jane Sweeney 1, 67br.

Bible Lands Museum Jerusalem: David Harris 41ca.

Bloomfield Science Museum: Avi Hayoun 48tl.

Design Museum Holon: Takumi Ota 40b.

Dreamstime.com: 34-5; Leonid Andronov 61tr; Antonella865 97b; Asafta 77bl; Beata Bar 16-7; Rafael Ben-ari 33crb, 84cla, 94b; Yehuda Bernstein 98t; Vladimir Blinov 33tl; Kobby Dagan 55tr; Dance60 63cl; Claudia Fernandes 103br; Evgeniy Fesenko 3tl, 14-5, 15crb, 15bl, 25tl, 27tl, 27br, 42tl, 50t, 64-5, 68-9, 69cla; 72cl, 81cra, 92bl, 92-3; Jaroslav Filsh 76clb; Steven Frame 30cla; Borya Galperin 43tr; Roberto Giovannini 90tl; Gkuna 30br; Rostislav Glinsky 13crb, 48-9; Kyrylo Glivin 10tr; Gorshkov13 17crb, 100cb; Hikrcn 76-7; Hugoht 46b, 88tc, 82-3; Ivgalis 47tl, 100tl; Jakich 34 -5; Jasmina 12cl, 28cra; Liorpt 10br, 54clb; Nitr 30-1; Ryszard Parys 63br, 78bl; Rndmst 91tr; Rostislavv 88-9; Rvc5pogod 6cb, 34bl; Jozef Sedmak 27cb, 43b, 66cla, 71tr; Serbysh 24-5; Elisei Shafer 99clb; Jacek Sopotnicki 10bl; Staselnik 45br; Suronin 26c; Aleksandar Todorovic 4clb, 35cr, 67tl; Ilia Torlin 35tl; Tsvibrav 75bl; Witr 102cl; Lu Yang 49cl, 97tr; Zatletic 11tc; Alevtina Zibareva 60b, 70b; Znm 96tl.

Getty Images: Ahmad Gharabli 14clb; Ulf Andersen 53cl; Atlantide Phototravel 13tl, 19crb, 21clb; Gonzalo Azumendi 2tl, 8-9; Walter Bibikow 85ca; Cosmo Condina 18clb, 61cl; Kevin Cullimore 50bl; Culture Club 38t; De Agostini / C. Sappa 102tr, 104c; Danita Delimont 24clb; Eddie Gerald 56t; GPO / Handout 53br; Handout 39tr; Robert Holmes 59tr; Hulton Archive 39cl; Hanan Isachar 44tl; Maremagnum 12-3; Nick Brundle Photography 56bl; Dan Porges 31tl; Guy Prives 86t; David Rubinger 52tl; Ilan Shacham 51tr, 51cl; Paul A. Souders 62bl; Space Images 16cla; George Steinmetz 46cla; Peter Unger 11br.

iStockphoto.com: liorpt 28-9; RnDmS 29cr.

The Norman: 58b, 87cl.

Rex Shutterstock: Omer Messinger 62t.

Robert Harding Picture Library: Schoening 4cl; Duby Tal 11crb.

Tel Aviv Museum of Art: Collection Moshe and Sara Mayer, Tel Aviv-Geneva/Edgar Degas *Scène de Ballet* ca. 188-1890, Pastel on paper, 65x94 cm. photo Avraham Hai 41crb.

Yad Vashem: 40tl.

Cover
Front and spine: **4Corners:** SIME / Luigi Vaccarella.

Back: **Dreamstime.com:** Ramblingman.

Pull Out Map Cover
4Corners: SIME / Luigi Vaccarella.

All other images © Dorling Kindersley
For further information see: www.dkimages.com

Penguin Random House

Printed and bound in China

First published in Great Britain in 2012
by Dorling Kindersley Limited
80 Strand, London WC2R 0RL

Copyright 2012, 2017 © Dorling Kindersley Limited

A Penguin Random House Company

17 18 19 20 10 9 8 7 6 5 4 3 2 1

Reprinted with revisions 2014, 2017

A CIP catalogue record is available from the British Library.

ISBN 978 0 2412 7900 7

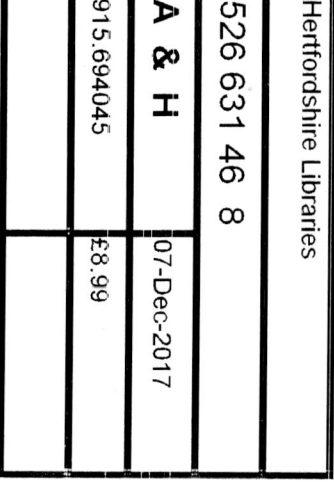

MIX
Paper from responsible sources
FSC™ C018179
www.fsc.org

SPECIAL EDITIONS OF DK TRAVEL GUIDES

DK Travel Guides can be purchased in bulk quantities at discounted prices for use in promotions or as premiums. We are also able to offer special editions and personalized jackets, corporate imprints, and excerpts from all of our books, tailored specifically to meet your own needs.

To find out more, please contact:

in the US
specialsales@dk.com

in the UK
travelguides@uk.dk.com

in Canada
specialmarkets@dk.com

in Australia
penguincorporatesales@ penguinrandomhouse.com.au

As a guide to abbreviations in visitor information blocks: **Adm** *= admission charge;* **DA** *= disabled access;* **D** *= dinner;* **L** *= lunch.*

Phrase Book

Hebrew Phrase Book

Hebrew has an alphabet of 22 letters. As in Arabic, the vowels do not appear in the written language and there are several systems of transliteration into Roman that are in use. In this phrase book we have provided only a simple and basic phonetic transliteration of the Hebrew word into the Roman alphabet. Bold type indicates the syllable on which the stress falls. An apostrophe between two letters means that there is a break in the pronunciation. The letters "kh" represent the sound "ch" as in Scottish "loch," and "g" is hard as in "gate." Where necessary, the masculine form is given first, followed by the feminine.

In an Emergency

Help!	Hatzilu!
Stop!	Atzor!
Call a doctor!	Azminu rofe!
Call an ambulance!	Azminu ambulans!
Call the police!	Tzaltzelu lamishtara!
Call the fire brigade!	Tzaltzelu lemekhabei esh!
Where is the nearest telephone?	Efo hatelefon hatziburi hakhi karov?
Where is the nearest hospital?	Efo bet hakholim hakhi karov?

Communication Essentials

Yes	Ken
No	Lo
Please	Bevakasha
Thank you	Toda
Excuse me	Slikha
Hello	Shalom
Good day	Boker tov
Greetings (on Shabbat)	Shabat Shalom
morning	boker
afternoon	akhar hatzohoryim
evening	erev
night	laila
today	hayom
tomorrow	makhar
here	po
there	sham
what?	ma?
which?	eizeh?
when?	matai?
who?	mi?
where?	efo?

Useful Phrases

How are you?	Ma shlomkha/ shlomekh?
Very well, thank you	Beseder, toda
Pleased to meet you	Na'immeod
Goodbye	Lehitraot
(I'm) fine	Beseder gamur
Where is/Where are?	Efo…?
How many kilometres is it to…?	Kama kilometrim mipo le…?
What is the way to…?	Ekh megi'im le…?
Do you speak English?	Ata/at medaber/ medaberet anglit?
I don't understand	Ani lo mevin/mevina

Useful Words

large	gadol
small	katan
hot	kham
cold	kar
bad	lo tov
enough	maspik
well	beseder
open	patuakh
closed	sagur
left	smol

right	yamin
straight	yashar
near	karov
far	rakhok
up	lemala
down	lemata
soon	mukdam
late	meukhar
entrance	knisa
exit	yetzia
toilet	sherutim
free, unoccupied	panui
free, no charge	khinam

Making a Telephone Call

I'd like to make a long-distance call	Haiti rotze/rotza lehitkasher lekhutz lair/laaretz
I'd like to make a reversed-charge call	Haiti rotze/rotza lehitkasher govaina
I'll call back later	Etkasher meukhar yoter
Can I leave a message?	Efshar lehashir hoda'a?
Hold on	Hamtin/hamtini (Tamtin/tamtini)
Could you speak up a little, please?	Tukhal/tukhli ledaber bekol ram yoter?
local call	sikha ironit
international call	sikha benleumit

Shopping

How much does it cost?	Kama zeh oleh?
I would like…	Haiti rotzeh/rotza…
Do you have…?	Yesh lakhem…?
I'm just looking.	Ani rak mistakel/ mistakelet.
Do you take credit cards?	Atem mekablim kartisei ashrai?
Do you take traveller's cheques?	Atem mekablim traveller's cheques?
What time do you open?	Matai potkhim?
What time do you close?	Matai sogrim?
this one	zeh
that one	hahu
expensive	Yakar
inexpensive/cheap	lo yakar/zol
size	mida

Staying in a Hotel

I have a reservation	Yesh li hazmana
Do you have a free room?	Yesh lakhem kheder panui?
double room	kheder zugi
room with two beds	kheder im shtei mitot
room with a bath or a shower	kheder im sherutim ve ambatia o miklakhat
single room	kheder yakhid
key	mafteakh
lift	ma'alit

Eating Out

Have you got a table free?	Yesh lakhem shulkhan panui?
I would like to book a table	Haiti rotze/rotza lehazmin shulkhan
The bill please	Kheshbon, bevakasha
I am vegetarian	Ani tzimkhoni/tzimkhonit
menu	tafrit
fixed-price menu	tafrit iskit
wine list	tafrit hayeinot
glass	kos
bottle	bakbuk
knife	sakin
spoon	kaf
fork	mazleg
breakfast	arukhat boker
lunch	arukhat tzohoryim
dinner	arukhat erev

Arabic Phrase Book

Transliteration from the Arabic script to the Roman alphabet is a difficult task. Although many attempts have been made, there is no satisfactory, consistent system. As a result, visitors will repeatedly come across contradictory spellings when traveling across the region. In this Arabic phrase book we have provided readers with only a simple and basic phonetic transliteration of the Arabic word or phrase into the Roman alphabet.

Pronunciation

a,-ah	as in "mad"
aa	as in "far"
aw	as in "law"
ay	as in "day"
e	as in "bed"
ee	as in "keen"
i	as in "bit"
o	as in "rob"
oo	as in "food"
u	as in "book"
A	pronounced as an emphasised "a," as in "both of us – you And me!"
D	a heavily pronounced "d"
gh	like a French "r" – from the back of the throat
H	a heavily pronounced "h"
kh	as in the Scottish pronunciation of "loch"
q	a "k" sound from the back of the mouth as in "caramel"
S,T	heavily pronounced "s", "t"
th	as in "thin"
Z	heavily pronounced "z"
'	this sounds like a small catch in the breath

In an Emergency

Help!	an-najdah!
Stop!	qeff!
I want to go to a doctor	oreed al zehab lel tabeeb
I want to go to a pharmacist	oreed al zehab lel saydaliya
Where is the nearest telephone?	ayn yoogad aqrab telifoon?
Where is the hospital?	ayn toogad al mostashfa?
I'm allergic to… penicillin/aspirin	Andee Hasaaseeyah men penicillin/aspirin

Communication Essentials

Yes/No	naAm/laa
Thank you	shokran
No, thank you	laa shokran
Please (asking for something)	min faDlak
Please (offering)	tafaDal
Good morning	sabaaH al-khayr
Good afternoon	as-salaam Alaykum
Good evening	masa' al-khayr
Good night	teSbaH Ala khayr (when going to bed)
Good night (leaving group early)	maA as-salaamah or as-salaam Alaykum
Goodbye	maA as-salaamah
Excuse me, please	min faDlak, law samaHt
today	al-yawm
yesterday	al-ams
tomorrow	ghadan
here	hona
there	honaak
what?	maza?
which?	ay?
when?	mata?
who?	man?
where?	ayn?

Useful Phrases

I don't understand	la afham
Do you speak English?	hal tatakalam engleezee?
I can't speak Arabic	la ataklam al Arabeya
I don't know	la aAref
My name is…	esmee…
How are you?	kayf Haalak?
Sorry!	aasef
Can you tell me…?	men fadlak qol lee…?
I would like…?	oreed…?
Is there…here?	yugad…hona?
Where can I get…?	ayn ajed…?
How much is it?	kam thaman haza (m) hazeehee (f)?
Do you take credit cards?	hal taqbal Visa/Access
Where is the toilet?	ayn ajed al-hamam?
left	yasaar
right	yameen
up	fawq
down	asfal

Travel

I want to go to…	oreed al zehab le…
How do you get to…?	kayf tazhab le…?
I'd like to rent a car	oreed asta'jer sayaarah
driver's licence	rokhSat qiyaadah
petrol/gas	banzeen
petrol/gas station	maHaTTat banzeen
When is there a flight to…?	mata toogad reHalat tayaran ela…?
What is the fare to…?	kam thaman al tazkarah le…?
A ticket to… please	law samaHt, tazkarat zehaab le…

Making a Telephone Call

May I use your telephone?	momken astaAmel teleefoonak?
How much is a call to…?	be-kam al-mokaalamah le…?
Can I call abroad from here?	momken ataSel bel-khaarej men hona?
My number is…	raqamee…
telephone call	mokaalamah
emergency	Tawaare'
operator	sentraal

Staying in a Hotel

Have you got any vacancies?	hal yoogad ghoraf khaaleeyah?
I have a reservation	Andee Hajz
I'd like a room with a bathroom	oreed ghorfah be-hammam
May I have the bill please?	momken al-hesab law samaHt?
I'll pay by credit card	sa-asfaA al-fatoorah law Visa/Access
I'll pay by cash	sa-adfaA naqdan
hotel	fondoq
air conditioning	takyeef
double room	ghorfa mozdawajah
single room	ghorfa be-sareer waaHed
shower	dosh
toilet	towaaleet
toilet paper	waraq towaleet
key	meftaaH
lift/elevator	mesAd
breakfast	foToor
restaurant	maTAm
bill	faatoorah

Selected Israel Index

Jerusalem Selected Street Index